Tn.A

This edition first published in Great Britain 2009 by
Crimson Publishing, a division of Crimson Business Ltd
Westminster House
Kew Road
Richmond
Surrey
TW9 2ND

A catalogue record for this book is available from the British
Library.

ISBN 978 1 90541 056 9

Printed and bound by LegoPrint SpA, Trento.

ACKNOWLEDGEMENTS

We owe our thanks to many people who have actively supported us while researching this book. We would particularly like to offer our sincere thanks to the parents who have contributed so honestly and for taking the time to share their experiences. Without the insight that they have provided into their lives we would not have been able to pass on their sound advice. We know from our research how demanding parenting a child with an additional need can be and fully appreciate them taking the time to discuss issues that can be emotionally draining.

We would also like to thank the professionals who offered their advice throughout the book. Particular thanks go to Ian Townsend who has acted as a sounding block and whose dedication to working with families continues to be an inspiration. Also many thanks to Lizzie Jenkins who works tirelessly to support families of children with disabilities and to promote understanding amongst professionals. Further thanks for their helpful input go to Relate counsellors Lynn Wilshaw and Joyce Wyke, counsellor and psychotherapist Carla Thompson, reflexologist Sarah Holland, Monica McCaffrey from Sibs, One Plus One, and Peter Burke of Hull University.

ABOUT THE AUTHORS

Victoria Dawson

Victoria Dawson has worked with children with special needs and their families for the last 10 years. She holds a Post Graduate Diploma in Special and Inclusive Education, a Diploma in Counselling and has also worked for Scope.

Antonia Chitty

Antonia Chitty is an experienced author and journalist who has worked in the field of visual impairment for a number of years, during which she has developed an understanding of issues around disability and having a child with special educational needs.

Contents

Introduction

Becoming a parent can be a difficult role to adjust to – and not just because babies don't come with a manual. Coping with your new arrival can put a strain on any couple's relationship, and when your child has an additional need this can add further pressures, both emotional and practical. Parents of children with special needs have to get to grips rapidly with hospital and social care systems and may have an uphill struggle to get their child the education they need. Your relationship can feel the strain as one parent becomes the main carer while the other needs to keep working. Money can be tight and you may seldom get the chance of a break. This all adds up to pressure on your relationship.

While writing this book we spoke to many parents to find their experiences of parenting a child with additional needs. Both mums and dads have shared with us the impact that bringing up their child has had on their relationship with their partner. It is on their thoughts and feelings that we have based our book.

Throughout the book you will find parents sharing the difficulties, challenges and joys that they have experienced throughout their parenting journey. There is also advice from experts. We have deliberately spoken to professionals who understand the additional strains and joys that living with a child with additional needs can bring. Some of these experts have children with special needs themselves.

We hope that by reading this book you will be encouraged to talk with your partner about your relationship. Continuing to talk is vital to getting through any challenging situation. This book will help you find out about how others in similar situations have coped. You will be able to benefit from the tips that they have offered so that your relationship can go from strength to strength.

THE WORDS WE USE

The language used around disability evolves over time. Many of the words that were socially acceptable in the 1960s are now seen as derogatory. Terms such as 'handicapped' are no longer used, as while someone may have a physical or mental impairment, they are only handicapped by society and the restrictive views of those around them. Some people today prefer to use the term 'disability' while others use alternative terms such as 'additional needs' or 'special needs'.

Throughout this book we use a variety of terms, taking the lead from the parents who took part in our research. All children are individuals and this is the same for children who have an additional need. When we talk about an 'additional need', a 'special need' or a disability we are discussing a difficulty that the child faces that may impair their functioning in some way.

It is important to recognise that just because a child in the book has a diagnosis of autism, they may not function in the same way as your child with autism. All children are truly individuals who may simply share a diagnosis. If you are unsure about advice in this book we recommend that you talk to your child's doctor, health visitor or other specialist in the relevant setting.

WHO SHOULD READ THIS BOOK?

This book will be useful for **parents** who have a child with an additional need in supporting their relationship. As authors we hope that you will find the words within these pages inspiring and will be able to empathise with the experience of others.

We also hope that the book will be useful for sharing with your **families and friends**. While others may sympathise, it often seems as though very few can actually understand your situation. If you see something in this book that rings true for you, use it to open up the subject with relatives and friends. It may then be easier for them to understand how you feel. By reading the stories that others share so honestly we hope that family and friends can be enlightened about how having a child with an additional need may impact upon you as a couple and how they can offer their support.

We also firmly believe that every **professional** who works with families of children with additional needs could benefit from reading this book. Parents voiced their concern throughout our research time and time again that professionals were not empathetic in their approach and did not understand the challenges that families face. This book aims to give an insight into the challenges in a positive manner, offering tips and advice for overcoming the many obstacles that are often put in the way of families.

Consider the huge range of professionals with whom families come into contact: paediatricians, teachers, social workers, consultants, physiotherapists, occupational therapists, speech and language therapists, not to mention a range of other therapists. It is clear to see that many families spend a great deal of time with professionals. It is therefore vital for professionals to understand holistically the issues that the families face if they are truly to work in partnership. We would encourage that you as parents recommend that the professionals you encounter read this book, particularly if you come across a professional who clearly doesn't understand your situation.

We also hope that our book will be read by **marriage and relationship guidance counsellors** so that when couples approach them for counselling they can have an understanding of the difficulties that may impact on the relationship. While there is much advice on improving a relationship that applies across the board, parenting a child with special needs creates unique and additional stresses. Understanding some of these pressures can help marriage guidance counsellors come up with relevant and manageable advice.

WHY IS THIS BOOK NEEDED?

Many parents report that they feel isolated when their child has an additional need and do not have anywhere to discuss the pressures on their relationship. While support groups exist, they tend to focus on emotional support. Although this is vital, it rarely extends to look at how parents are getting on together. And groups are often only attended by one parent due to practical constraints of work and caring. This book aims to support both parents as a couple. We hope that by reading others' accounts you will feel less isolated and will use the book as a vehicle for opening up communication within your relationship.

Information can be difficult to access. This book aims to be user-friendly and offer you simple tips to try that are effective. As well as parents, professionals have contributed throughout the book in order to offer their best tips and most practical advice to help with a range of situations. We also highlight useful organisations and where to find more help.

A happy relationship benefits the whole family and can ease some of the stress involved with parenting a child with a disability. We thrive on building relationships and when they are working positively these can help to promote our wellbeing. It is therefore essential that these relationships are looked after.

THE RESEARCH WE USED

Contact a Family is a national charity which has conducted research into how having a child with an additional need impacted on couples' relationships. It surveyed over 2,000 parents from a wide range of backgrounds to find out the issues that they were facing. The findings suggested that parents faced feelings of isolation and there were many issues that impacted on their lives including:

- Having little time to spend together
- Financial pressures
- Employment difficulties
- Lack of support and understanding from professionals

The research highlighted that those couples parenting a child with a disability are at greater risk of developing issues within their relationship due to the added pressures that they face.

Contact a Family has worked alongside One Plus One, a research charity, to produce a guide to relationships and parenting a disabled child. Details of this guide, which is full of advice from parents, are available in the help list on page 187. The research that Contact a Family has carried out and the information that parents shared highlighted the need for this book, which will take a detailed look at relationships.

During our own research we have spoken to a wide range of parents. The one thing they have in common is that they are all parents of children with disabilities. We have spoken to parents who are part of a couple, those who are divorced and those who are single. We have spoken to fathers who are often overlooked when it comes to parenting. Parents were keen to share their stories and many approached us when they heard about our proposal for this book. All of our interviewees wanted to pass on information that may potentially help other parents to strengthen their relationships.

We have also spoken to professionals, ranging from clinical psychologists to counsellors and researchers. We have included their ideas throughout our book using their specialist knowledge to underpin the advice that is given.

Throughout this book we have mentioned many helpful organisations. You can find a full list and contact details at the back of the book.

IN SUMMARY

We hope that you will find the book interesting and that you will be able to identify with the issues that are dealt with. Above all, we hope that by sharing the stories of other parents any isolation that you might feel will be reduced. This book can be used in order to promote communication between couples and families and to strengthen family relationships benefiting each member, including your child.

1

A baby changes everything

In this chapter

- The impact of the new arrival

- Becoming mummy and daddy: changing roles

- Babies with health problems

- Long-distance parenting and hospital stays

- Nurturing your relationship through the loss of a child

- Sex life and babies

- The effect on friendships

- Maintaining your relationship

Having a baby is a life-changing experience. Nothing is ever quite the same again. While it can be a wonderful experience there is no doubt that it presents parents with challenges. New parents can find that their finances are under considerable strain with one partner often having to give up work for the short term at least: if you have a child with special needs you may suddenly be faced with one parent becoming a carer in the long term.

For all parents, leisure time can be a thing of the past and is often substituted by feeding, nappy-changing and washing. If your child has special needs this can become more demanding, with the need for nappies and frequent changes of clothes extending beyond when you expect.

The roles in the relationship between parents can also alter now that there is a baby on the scene. This chapter looks at the issues that you may face as a new parent, as well as a parent of a child with special needs, and how this impacts on your relationship with your partner.

At the baby and toddler stage some parents may have just got an initial diagnosis, while many do not know about their child's additional needs or are only beginning to suspect that their child is not developing as expected. Others may have already spent months with their newborn in a special care unit, dealing with the demands of long-distance parenting. If your child is already embroiled in a series of operations to deal with congenital problems you may feel ill-prepared for making decisions that will have lifelong implications. The worries about what decisions to make can cause rifts between parents as you struggle to adjust your ideas about your child, which developed while he or she was in the womb, to reality after their birth.

However, many of the struggles of early parenthood are similar whether your child has special needs or not, and even the closest relationships can be put to the test. But if you are finding parenthood difficult, you are not alone.

> Having a baby is life-changing. Most couples cannot imagine the impact that having a baby will have on their lives, let alone their relationship, until it happens.
>
> Lynn Wilshaw, Relate counsellor

Read on for advice from other parents about how they survived their baby's first year.

THE IMPACT OF THE NEW ARRIVAL

Whether or not your newborn has been identified as having an additional need, parenthood is hard work. While the adverts show babies looking cute and fast asleep in fluffy towels that are freshly laundered, the reality is often far different. The change from being a childless couple to parenthood is a shock to your system.

> Parenthood is a lot more taxing than I ever imagined. I didn't realise it would make me so temperamental, anxious and stressed.
>
> Julie, mother of two

Babies are incredibly hard work, creating a never-ending washing pile, filling nappies at an alarming rate and demanding feeds at inconvenient moments.

With parenthood comes a responsibility that is almost overwhelming. I found it difficult to adjust to having to be at the complete command of a small baby and tiring beyond imagination. I have never before experienced the exhaustion of sleepless nights and I found it incredibly hard to function.

Suzanne, mother of two daughters

It is little wonder that more than fifty per cent of new mums suffer from depression in those early days. In addition to the work that babies create they are also incredibly expensive considering their size. Starting a family often puts a financial strain on couples which in turn can impact on the relationship.

I felt under enormous pressure to get back to work as soon as possible after the birth. I am the main wage earner in our home and we couldn't afford for me to not be earning. I went back to full-time work when Rueben was six weeks old. It is the hardest thing I've ever done. He woke several times each night and I had to get up to feed him, manage running the home and hold down a responsible job. Looking back I don't know how I did it — it was exhausting.

Sarah

If one parent takes time off work to look after their child, this can lead to feelings of social isolation.

I 've always been career minded and when I had Charlie I took maternity leave. I hate to say it but I was so low, I missed the buzz of the office, the conversation, the social life that went with it. I felt very lonely during those first few months.

Zoe

The isolation can be compounded when your partner gets home from work and seems to fail to understand the struggles you have had to simply feed and dress yourself and the baby. Both of you can end up angry and resentful that the other one has the easier job.

If you are feeling lonely it may be worth speaking to your health visitor about baby groups that are running in your area. They are an excellent way to make friends with other new parents and will also offer your baby stimulating play opportunities. It can seem hard to get out of the house, and you may worry that no-one will speak to you. Persevere, try a few different groups and you are sure to find some new friends who are in the same boat. Home dads can find it even harder to find other men who are the main carer, but there are usually a few around, so do join groups even if they seem full of women at first.

Unfortunately, parents who have a child with an additional need can face these issues throughout their child's life, whereas the majority of new parents can be secure in the knowledge that this stage will be short-lived. Many parents whom we spoke to during our research, however, reported that due to their child's needs issues such as sleep deprivation, financial difficulties and feelings of isolation continued throughout their child's life.

BECOMING MUMMY AND DADDY: CHANGING ROLES

Becoming parents sees a change in your roles and in your personal identities. Suddenly you lose your own name and become 'Jack's mummy' or 'Fiona's daddy'. This can also impact on your relationship with your partner. You will now see each other in your new roles as parents and it is important that you talk to each other during this time of transition so that you still see each other as lovers too.

Avoid calling each other 'mummy' and 'daddy' but use your partner's name to ensure that your identities as lovers are preserved.

When my daughter was born I felt completely rejected by my wife. It was as though my job was done now, thank you very much. Sharon was obsessed by the baby. I couldn't touch our daughter without being told I was doing it wrong. Sharon had no time for me or us, it was all baby talk. I'm pleased to say things have got better but Sharon now wants another child and I'm just not sure I can go there again.

David

David's story isn't uncommon. Many dads report feeling rejected by their partners following the birth of a baby. Lynn Wilshaw of Relate confirms this and says, 'Men can sometimes feel rejected by their partners who may appear to give all their affection to the baby.'

> I realised the second I set eyes on my baby that the feelings I had were of absolute love, I was besotted. For a long time I found it hard to let my husband be involved. I realise this sounds very strange but for a period he was surplus to requirements. I was concentrating so much on the care of my baby that he came very low on my list of priorities.
>
> Suzanne

Often the scenarios that we have heard above lessen over time as a child becomes less dependent.

> Jay has been very mummy-centred. This has made it difficult at weekends when he used to howl if left with his dad. Now he is two he talks more about Daddy, asks about him when he is at work, and looks forward to doing things with him at the weekends.
>
> Nell

If your child has additional needs, they may be dependent for care for more than a few years, and this exclusion of one parent, usually the father, can continue. If this is the case in your family, here are some suggestions to redress the balance:

- It is important that you talk openly to each other about parenting your child and explain if you feel excluded.

- On the other hand, you may want to explain to your partner that you feel you have the lion's share of the care and would like to do less on occasion.

- You may want to negotiate special jobs that are your responsibility alone so that you do feel that you are having an input into your child's care.

- Alternatively, if there are some jobs that both of you find difficult, make a rota. This may mean that mum does more during the week, and dad takes over for some of the weekend.

Often, one parent is anxious that the other cannot perform a task as well as necessary. This is natural when some jobs may cause your child to become agitated: the more experienced parent will be quicker and more adept at minimising distress. You need to discuss this in a calm manner rather than become critical of each other's attempts. Spend some time showing each other the best way to feed your child, bathe them and so on. Remember your partner is as keen to care for your child as you are so allow them the opportunity. It is essential for the bonding process. You will both benefit in the long term, but may need a lot of patience to make the change.

BABIES WITH HEALTH PROBLEMS

Most parents expect that their child will be born perfect. If you are informed at a scan that your child has a chance of having a congenital condition it can be a shock. You will go through similar emotions including grief, anger and denial if a problem emerges after your child is born. This can cause conflict between you and your partner if, as is likely, you experience different emotions at different times. If you are feeling anger while your partner is tired and weepy after a difficult birth and mainly feeling grief for the loss of the perfect baby she expected, it can be hard to relate.

Most hospitals will be able to put you in touch with a counsellor who can help you talk through some of the issues that come up when your baby is born with a health condition.

One of the issues that may arise at this stage is how much medical intervention you want for your child. With a sick baby you are suddenly put in the position of making decisions for the long term for which you feel ill-prepared. Sometimes you will have to make a rapid decision, but at other times you may have some days to think about your options and the implications for your baby. Don't be afraid to ask to speak to the medics in charge of your baby if you are unclear or unsure.

We were shocked, upset and scared. I'd suggest that other couples in this situation go back to the consultant together to really talk it through.

Arabella

It can be helpful to get in touch with Contact a Family to see if you can talk to other parents who have been in the same situation.

Talking to a counsellor can also help you get things straight in your own mind. A third person can help when you and your partner have different perspectives too.

You can make a request for an Early Support package to be put into place for your family. Early Support is a government initiative which helps you work alongside professionals to develop a family plan. Contact details for the Early Support project can be found on page 195.

LONG-DISTANCE PARENTING AND HOSPITAL STAYS

There are practical difficulties if your baby needs to stay in hospital. If it is your firstborn you may be juggling the need to hold on to your job with the need to support each other. It can be extremely stressful whether you are the one who stays in the hospital or the one who has to go out and carry on some semblance of normal life.

If you have a sick child, ask for compassionate leave so you have some time to get through a difficult period together.

When the only special care baby unit is some distance away and you are faced with the possibility of months away from home, things can seem extra hard. It can take time to work out accommodation: the hospital is the best place to start to ask for help with this as they may know what other parents have done.

Ronald McDonald House Charities provide 12 Ronald McDonald houses close to hospitals and 29 sets of Ronald McDonald family rooms in hospitals across the UK so parents can stay close to their child. The Sick Children's Trust is another organisation offering accommodation near to children's hospitals.

If you have other children, things can get even more complex. Family and friends may be able to help, but the burden on you as parents can leave you both feeling torn in two.

> Jay was in hospital when he was four months old. Our daughter was just four. David and I took turns to dash to and from the hospital so one of us was with each child. We did alternate nights at home and in hospital where one of us slept on a couch alongside Jay's cot. We relied on friends to cover the travel time. I was still breastfeeding, but Jay was too ill to take milk from the breast so I had to fit in expressing too.
>
> Nell

NURTURING YOUR RELATIONSHIP THROUGH THE LOSS OF A CHILD

Kurt and Karen's story

Kurt and Karen's son Jack had complex needs. As well as spina bifida and chromosome 18q syndrome he had chronic lung disease and required oxygen and a feeding tube. The couple had a team of five nurses working in their home to meet Jack's needs. Sadly, Jack passed away when he was almost three years old but here the couple share their experience of parenting their son and how they kept their relationship strong. The couple also have two other sons.

We took Jack's doctor's advice to heart and 'guarded our marriage' throughout Jack's life and after his death. Jack's doctor was fantastic: he even gave us the statistics on marriage break-ups when the couple have a child with special needs. About two months after Jack was born he really encouraged us to take the boys and go away for the weekend. He told us Jack had the best care in the hospital with nurses at his side and he would call us if anything came up. We took his advice and went to a local hotel with a water park for the weekend. It was really good for the four of us.

As a couple we are both committed to our marriage and knew we had more going against us having Jack and then losing him. Divorce is not an option for either of us. I believe that the best thing you can do for your child is to make your marriage stay strong. I know that doesn't always happen, though. Kurt is an amazing husband and father. There was never anything he wouldn't do with Jack. He did everything that I did and the nurses did. He's always been very involved with our boys and never shied away from doing what needed to be done. You need to be a team and help each other.

Karen

The additional difficulties created more pressure but you can choose how you react to these. We chose to deal with the difficulties in such a way that it brought us closer together. Selfishness is the root of most relationship problems so it is important to be willing to give up something you enjoy — and this may include wanting to be right! It is more important to find what is best for your family. Spend time together with your partner doing things you both like. Given the restraints of children this may be as simple as watching TV, a film at home or reading in the same room.

Kurt

As a couple Karen and Kurt have recognised the need for spending quality time together.

We have always been fairly regimented about bedtime for our sons, because once they are in bed it's our time together. We tell them frequently that we need our time to talk and unwind, so they need to go to bed and stay there. We also have dinner as a family at least five nights a week.

Karen

The couple also recognise that they had different roles in Jack's life which helped them to work as an effective team.

I was the one who dealt with nurses, doctors, teachers and social workers and the day to day detail of Jack's life.

Karen

Yes, we had different roles. Karen worked at home to take care of Jack and our other sons while I continued to go to work to provide for the family. We both did what we could to provide the best care for our children out of the common love we share for them.

Kurt

A mutual respect for each other's role is key to maintaining a healthy relationship.

At times couples do deal with the emotion of parenting a child with an additional need in different ways.

As difficult as it is to admit that your child needs help, work through the denial as quickly as possible. Trust your doctor or whoever gives the diagnosis and get on with helping your child. Your denial does not change the truth. There can be tremendous joys ahead that you would never have imagined. Yes, you may not realise some of your old dreams, but you will have new ones and they will be even more satisfying when they come true.

Kurt

When Jack passed away Karen saw a bereavement counsellor. She noticed that Kurt didn't cry as much as she did.

> I wanted to know that Kurt was grieving 'properly'. The counsellor thought he was doing fine and asked, 'Would you really want him to cry as much as you do?' Of course we grieved differently because we are different.
>
> Karen

SEX LIFE AND BABIES

Sex and newborn babies do not generally go together terribly well. Women are often sore after the birth and it may take some time for normal desires to resume. What is more, night time is no longer your own.

> Feelings of exhaustion coupled with feelings of failure can lead to tension between the couple and if you aren't careful this can lead to blame and the partners becoming distant.
>
> Lynn Wilshaw, Relate counsellor

> It took me quite a while to get back into sex after the births of both my children — six months I'd say. It is now as good as ever though, and even if we did have the energy to swing from the chandeliers, we probably wouldn't want to risk it in case one of them walked in on us.
>
> Diana

Women report that they feel less sexy after having a baby due to changes in their body shape. Spare tyres, shrinking boobs and stretch marks were all mentioned by new mums when asked about how motherhood had physically changed them.

I had a vaginal birth and needed lots of stitches afterwards. I was afraid to have sex in case everything hadn't healed and to be honest I really didn't feel at all sexy. I wondered if my husband would ever fancy sex again after what he saw during labour. Luckily he did.

Rebecca

Share your concerns about your body with your partner. Men's responses to these worries can be enlightening.

My wife is always complaining about the stretch marks that she got when carrying our son. I love them. They are a part of her that she got from carrying our child and there is something very special about that. It doesn't put me off in the least, she is beautiful just as she is.

Robert

Women often don't feel very keen on sex and this can intensify the feelings of rejection. Generally, women start getting their desire back within a few months of having a baby. If this doesn't happen, then maybe a chat with the doctor or family planning workers would help. They are used to seeing this problem regularly so there is no need to be embarrassed.

Lynn Wilshaw, Relate counsellor

Additional factors, such as dealing with the shock of an unexpected diagnosis, can have implication for your sex life too. Stress of any sort can affect the chemicals in your body that make you feel sexy: your body is using all its resources to cope with the challenges you are facing and sex becomes an unnecessary extra. It can be hard to get out of this situation and may take some conscious effort to get things going again.

Take time to cuddle and be close without any pressure to have penetrative sex. Make one night a week a time for a takeaway, a bottle of wine, a good film or perhaps cook a new dish and enjoy eating it together.

Even if it is hard to get a babysitter because of your circumstances a 'date night' can help you remember that you are a couple, not just parents who have just found out that their child has special needs.

THE EFFECT ON FRIENDSHIPS

Friendships can be affected by the birth of a baby, whether or not your child has special needs.

Fellow parents are fine but childless friends have all fallen by the wayside.

Louise

This seems to be a common theme with childless friends often not understanding the pressures of parenthood.

My friends that don't have children think they can just call me at 7pm and invite me to meet them at 8pm. They have no concept of childcare. Now they don't invite me as often because I usually have to say no.

Chloe

We have new friends now who we have met through having children.

Yvette

If you don't see old friends as often as you like, invite them over to your house for a meal, or have a takeaway if you can't face cooking. Alternatively, have people over for a night of games that will get you all laughing. Explain to your friends that you can't go out but that you would love to see them on a regular basis at your home.

I have lots more friends after having children, all of whom I have motherhood in common with. It can be a very strong bond. My social life is probably better now than at any point because I have lots of 'mums' nights out' and they are often

25

quite wild as we have more tension to release. The few friends I have who haven't had kids tend to have dropped by the wayside a bit, which is a shame but rather inevitable as kids do dominate your life.

Charlotte

MAINTAINING YOUR RELATIONSHIP

So how do you successfully maintain your relationship with your partner as well as being parents?

This is a period of adjustment and you have to realise that things do change beyond recognition from the relationship that you had together before children. Make sure that you do things together that are fun and nothing to do solely with work or children

Suzanne

Praise each other's efforts with your child. It is far too easy to be critical and not to acknowledge the good parenting that each of you is carrying out.

Keep in contact with friends and take it in turns to babysit so that you can have some nights free on a regular basis. Ask family if they would be prepared to babysit for you every so often so that you can have some quality time as a couple. Lynn Wilshaw works with new parents on a regular basis.

Try to spend some 'couple time' together without the baby if possible. Don't be afraid to ask grandparents to babysit — they are often only too willing to do so. You need to take care of your relationship so that you can both take care of your child. Try not to blame each other when things go wrong. Act as a couple, work together and remember you are not the only ones facing the problem. It will get better, but you both need time to adjust.

Lynn Wilshaw, Relate counsellor

IN SUMMARY

Parenting can be a demanding job particularly when you have a young baby. When your baby has additional needs the strain can be magnified. Becoming a parent can impact on your relationship with your partner and with your friends. If you are taking maternity or paternity leave it can also leave you feeling socially isolated from colleagues at work. It is important that you communicate as a couple and share your worries and stresses. It is hard to tell when you are doing well, and, like many parents, you may feel you are just stumbling from one day to the next. Make time to celebrate the little things that go well, even when times are difficult.

2

Acknowledging a special need

In this chapter

- Parents' experiences of diagnosis
- Having different feelings from your partner
- How counselling can help
- The impact on your future
- The world of professionals
- Accepting the diagnosis
- Dealing with parental conflict
- Our helpful friend 'denial'
- Understanding your coping strategies
- Other members of the family
- Acknowledgement versus acceptance
- Receiving a diagnosis and dealing with it together

Finding out that your child has a special need can be a devastating experience for you and for your wider family. Whoever said that motherhood came with a huge helping of guilt was spot on. Many mothers that we have spoken to reported looking to themselves as being the cause of their child's special need. Women question whether something that they had done in pregnancy could have caused the difficulty. Some dads said that they have felt a sense of failure. Many told us that they felt they were unable to talk to anybody about their true feelings. Men often throw themselves into their work.

Tracey's son was born with a visual impairment which was not discovered until he was two.

Reassurance from the medical experts that I was not to blame did not help. Looking back, I was in shock, desperately searching for reasons and answers. Well-meaning family members asked if it could be down to me having a minor operation during pregnancy which again set me off on the path of self-blame. Then they delved into the family tree, searching for anybody else who may have had eye problems to attribute the blame to. I needed to know why Jake's eye condition had arisen and so did my family. Somehow, though, they forgot my feelings in their search for answers.

Tracey

PARENTS' EXPERIENCES OF DIAGNOSIS

Parents' experience of diagnosis seems to be very mixed. If your child's condition is as yet undiagnosed, or seems not to have a name, you may feel that having a label for the condition could help you to become better informed and move on. On the other hand, a diagnosis can lead to worries about your child being labelled. It may open up new concerns for you about further problems related to the condition your child has been diagnosed with, as you search for further information.

Many parents speak of how they found professionals insensitive in the way they delivered a diagnosis.

It is overwhelmingly clear that there is not enough emotional support offered to parents around the time of diagnosis. Dealing with stressful news without any back-up can drive you and your partner apart just at the time when you need to be able to support each other.

You may be aware that your child will have a special need before the birth.

> We were told that our baby probably wouldn't make it to birth and advised over and over to terminate him. This wasn't an option for me and even when he was born I felt that I had to fight the doctors in order to keep him alive. I was determined to keep our baby. If he died it would be under his own steam. My husband considered

termination and we spent hours talking about this. Eventually he agreed that it wasn't an option for us. The best advice I can give couples going through a similar thing is to talk. Saying things out loud makes it more real.

Sharon, whose baby was born in
the Netherlands

Jean's daughter was born at 42 weeks' gestation with cerebral palsy due to clinical negligence.

I was in denial for several years. Initially we wanted revenge and to get justice for our little girl.

Jean

In Jean's case it was her solicitor who first spoke to the family about the likelihood of a diagnosis of cerebral palsy. When they consulted the medics about this at their daughter's assessment it was confirmed.

Jess also describes difficulty in getting a diagnosis for her daughter, Eleanor.

The medics seemed to not want to label my daughter's condition. It was another mum who mentioned cerebral palsy, and it was up to me to ask the consultant if this was what was affecting Eleanor. When it was diagnosed I thought we were just attending a routine appointment — my husband was at work so I went with my mother-in-law.

Jess

Receiving a suggested diagnosis unexpectedly can be doubly stressful. Friends and other professionals who suggest a diagnosis which sounds likely are not going to be equipped to support you with more details, and you may be left wondering where to go for help and support.

Speak to your consultant as soon as possible about the possible diagnosis, and call Contact a Family for help to access good quality resources on many conditions.

Some parents describe being given a diagnosis as a relief. They found it helpful to have a name for their child's condition.

When Charlie was diagnosed as having Asperger's syndrome it helped Dave to change his views. He could then see that the behaviour wasn't Charlie's fault. It was the Asperger's kicking in. We were both expecting the diagnosis but hadn't fully anticipated the relief that we would feel from receiving it. On balance I would say our relationship became closer, but then it was extremely strong anyway. I think had it not been as strong, then having a child with an additional need could have driven us further apart.

Julia

HAVING DIFFERENT FEELINGS FROM YOUR PARTNER

Do not expect that you and your partner will take a diagnosis in the same way. You may have different feelings at different times: one of you may deny that your child has a problem, while the other is experiencing feelings of intense grief. This in itself can often lead couples into crisis as it is easy to think that because your partner isn't sharing your feelings, they don't care.

> I sobbed, cried and grieved for the 'normal' child that I wasn't going to have. I blamed myself as it must have been something I did. I cried for my beautiful boy who was going to have to face so much and I wished it were someone else's child and not mine. My husband refused to accept the diagnosis, insisting that the experts were wrong. It took an incident where he was playing football at the park with our son to make him acknowledge that he is autistic. They'd been playing quite happily when a childminder arrived with several children. As soon as they approached, our son threw a hissy fit and got in his buggy, strapping himself in to go home. My husband came home distraught and said, 'He is autistic isn't he?'
>
> Suzi

It is important to talk about your feelings with your partner. No two people are going to feel the same and just because your partner is reacting in a different way from you doesn't mean that they aren't hurting. Men and women generally communicate very differently. Women tend to be more open with their emotions and discuss how they are feeling. Men, however, tend to function more as problem-solvers and may become frustrated if they cannot provide a solution to the child's disability.

HOW COUNSELLING CAN HELP

Counselling can help couples to explore their feelings in a safe and secure environment which will allow you to strengthen your relationship. If you feel that your relationship needs support you could ask your GP to refer you to a counsellor. Waiting lists, however, are often long. Some companies offer employees free counselling. Contact your HR department and see if this is an option. Alternatively, you could pay to see a counsellor privately.

Disability in families can have a ripple effect on the whole family. Individuals often experience a sense of grief or self-blame or maybe loss of personal identity. Maintaining life as a couple can be very difficult when caring for a disabled child. Counselling at any stage can help individuals and couples explore and understand their own and their partner's feelings. It is never about advice, since practical information can be accessed elsewhere, but about the emotional effect of change.

The sessions can address the way couples communicate and support each other and enhance these skills. It can enable couples to attain a better balance between caring for all the children in the family and having time for themselves. Individual expectations and ways to resolve conflict are also important. Partners or individuals can think about their lives now and explore what changes they want to make and how to achieve them.

Joyce Wike, Relate counsellor

Joyce also highlights the importance of finding the right counsellor for you as a couple.

In looking for a suitable counsellor don't be afraid to ask questions about the counsellor's qualifications, areas of interest or experience and training in couple or family therapy. Only you can decide which practitioner feels right for you. Ask yourself whether you feel comfortable talking to them? Do you like their manner? Could you be open with them?

Joyce Wike, Relate counsellor

Talking to a third party can be difficult at first and it is important that you and your partner chose somebody that you feel comfortable speaking with. Sometimes it can help to write down notes prior to a meeting. You could include:

- Your thoughts before you attend
- What you hope to get out of the sessions
- Some of your feelings around the situation

Sometimes it can be too difficult to talk about issues, so if you are finding it difficult to open up, explain this to your counsellor and they may be able to offer you alternative ideas to help you to broach subjects, such as writing your feelings down in a letter or expressing your feelings through drawings.

THE IMPACT ON YOUR FUTURE

Angela's daughter received a diagnosis of cerebral palsy at 14 months.

> I was devastated at the impact the diagnosis had on our future as a family. We had always wanted to have four children yet after the diagnosis my husband wanted to give all our attention to Lydia, whereas I wanted to have another child to take the pressure off her.
>
> Angela

Receiving the difficult news that your child has an additional need can impact on your lives for many years. It is not uncommon for parents to have planned a life together, mapping out their dreams. At the time of diagnosis it can feel as though these dreams have been shattered and a new plan needs to be drawn up. Consider as a couple how you can work on taking small steps towards putting a new life plan together. Take time to talk to each other about the disappointment that you feel around your lives. Make sure that you also talk about the good things in your life as it is now. Once you start looking for the positives there are usually more than you might have thought there would be.

This may not have been the route you both expected your life to take but it can be a positive one if you support each other, communicate and plan together.

> We were not given our own space to come to terms with what was happening at diagnosis. I still don't know what my husband thought at the time. We have since split up. In the long term he obviously needed to talk, but not with me.
>
> Jane

THE WORLD OF PROFESSIONALS

More complex conditions can lead you into a world full of professionals. One child can be seen by several specialists including:

- Speech and language therapist
- Physiotherapist
- Occupational therapist
- Paediatrician
- Health visitor
- Specialist teacher
- Portage worker
- Educational psychologist

There is little wonder that parents sometimes feel that their home has been taken over by professionals and equipment. It is important that as a couple you have your own space to come to terms with the diagnosis.

Ask professionals if they can do joint visits to your child to cut down the number of visits that take place. Similarly, if you have numerous hospital appointments speak to your therapists, or key worker if you have one, about co-ordinating them to reduce the number of visits you have to make.

ACCEPTING THE DIAGNOSIS

Parents may have very different ideas regarding whether to accept a diagnosis. Rachel's son received a diagnosis of Tourette's syndrome and obsessive-compulsive disorder. The family, however, chose not to have the diagnosis recorded as Rachel's husband felt that it would label the child.

It was a major mistake not to have the diagnosis officially recorded. There is no support now for my son — he is unemployable but gets no benefits either. I am angry that I listened to my husband. My son is from a previous relationship and I'm also angry that my husband has had such a huge input into my child's life when the child is not his own. He can be so critical of my son. Having a child with an additional need has caused me a lot of stress. It puts pressure on several relationships, not just the one with my husband.

Rachel

If you are facing a similar situation it is important to sit down with your partner and discuss the implications a diagnosis may have on the family. Write down all the positives that may come from gaining a diagnosis, such as the fact you will be able to research the condition, meet other parents in similar situations and gain additional help with schooling if necessary. Then write down the reasons why a diagnosis may be detrimental to your family. You may include things such as not wanting your child to be labelled and your concern about how a diagnosis might affect their future.

Use the list below to get you started, and then add your own ideas together. You may wish to carry out this exercise individually at first. Once you have compiled your list, leave it for 24 hours. Then read through it again and make any amendments or additions. You may then feel that it is time for you to share the list with your partner. This exercise will support you in speaking honestly about your feelings around diagnosis. Listen to your partner's feelings and concerns about getting a diagnosis: just saying them out loud can help.

Pros	Cons
● Easier to research the condition	● The risk of being labelled
● Easier to find other parents in similar situations	● A label might limit what people expect from my child
● May get additional help with schooling	● Other problems might be missed
● Easier to explain to other people	● One of us may not want or accept the diagnosis
● May get financial help	

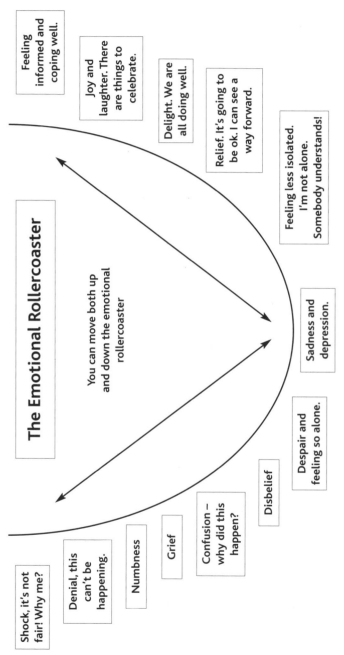

The Emotional Rollercoaster

You can move both up and down the emotional rollercoaster

Feeling informed and coping well.

Joy and laughter. There are things to celebrate.

Delight. We are all doing well.

Relief. It's going to be ok. I can see a way forward.

Feeling less isolated. I'm not alone. Somebody understands!

Sadness and depression.

Despair and feeling so alone.

Disbelief

Confusion – why did this happen?

Grief

Numbness

Denial, this can't be happening.

Shock, it's not fair! Why me?

Thanks to Scope for allowing us to use and adapt their transitional rollercoaster model as featured in their Strengthening Families Training Package.

DEALING WITH PARENTAL CONFLICT

Rachel's experience where she and her husband wanted different things for their child is very common. When you are talking about your child and their needs, emotions can run high. It is important to remember that you both want what is best for your child, but sometimes you may not share the same vision.

Many parents have described having a child with an additional need as being like a rollercoaster ride of emotion. Scope's 'Strengthening Families' training package uses a rollercoaster model so that parents can identify where they are emotionally at a given time. Scope has kindly allowed us to use an adapted version of this model. The diagram overleaf shows the range of emotions that parents may go through. What is interesting to note is that parents report that you can move forwards through the emotions but you can also move backwards. One parent said she had felt that she had moved through the emotions after diagnosis and was coping well, yet when her child could not walk and was fitted for her first wheelchair, she immediately went back to the beginning of the cycle of emotion.

A useful exercise is to spend some time contemplating where you are emotionally at the moment, using the diagram. Then ask your partner to identify where they are. Talk through the feelings you have each identified, and you will find this makes it easier to see where the other is emotionally. Sometimes, if one partner is still feeling guilt while the other has moved through the emotion range, it can be easy for arguments to occur. The partner who is feeling guilty may not be able to understand why the other partner is going about their everyday life with some normality.

You may believe that your partner doesn't care or isn't hurting the way you are. Using the diagram will help you to see that couples do experience things differently on an emotional level but these feelings are still important and need to be understood.

OUR HELPFUL FRIEND 'DENIAL'

Shirley Young is the mother of two adult sons who both have additional needs. She has worked as director of a voluntary agency supporting parents of disabled children. Shirley has written an essay about coping strategies that was published in *Family-centred Support for Children with Disabilities and Special Needs* (Interconnections, 2007).

I feel that denial can be an extremely useful and effective coping mechanism when used appropriately, both for parents and for the professionals who work with them, but seriously damaging when used beyond usefulness and left unchallenged.

Shirley Young, expert on coping strategies

Denial can be one of the most helpful but least understood coping strategies. It is a powerful defence used in traumatic circumstances. Denial can be useful in that it allows you to get out of bed in the morning and function with some degree of normality. It can help to protect you from dealing with difficult feelings that you do not feel ready to tackle.

At times denial does need to be sensitively challenged. It may be necessary to make decisions about your child which require you to leave your state of denial. For example, when considering the future of a child with profound and multiple difficulties one parent we spoke to accepted that she was in denial about the future and it was far too difficult to even begin to think about. With time moving on, however, it became necessary for her to deal with this situation and to make provision for the future. She needed to be sensitively supported in order to acknowledge the situation that was facing her and her child.

Ask a professional who you feel comfortable with to help you talk through issues if you know there is something you just can't face dealing with.

UNDERSTANDING YOUR COPING STRATEGIES

Are you able to identify what your coping strategies are? They may vary enormously from person to person and could include things such as focusing intensely on your child, researching your child's condition so you know all about it on an intellectual level, or having a strong faith.

When everything gets too much, I tend to bury myself in work. It is something that I can control, when everything else seems out of control. My partner buries himself in work too, which can mean we don't get to talk about issues when we really should.

Nell

Talk to your partner about coping strategies and what you each use. You will see that you cope in very different ways, which at times may lead to conflict. Understanding that these are coping mechanisms should help to reduce conflict and help you to strengthen your relationship.

Consider what you do in the following situations. You may be able to identify where you are on the cycle of emotion during different situations. Read the examples, then make a copy to fill in for yourself. Your partner may want to do one too.

Example:

When I'm sad	I want to be given time to cry and not for you to tell me that everything will be all right.
When I'm angry	I find something that needs cleaning and put all my energy into that.
When I get difficult news about our child	I go quiet. I'm thinking and trying to acknowledge what has been said. I'm not ignoring you.
When I have to attend a meeting/ appointment about our child	I get nervous and can become snappy with you.
When I'm frustrated	I feel cross inside and need to vent my frustrations to someone who understands.

Your feelings:

When I'm sad	I ....
When I'm angry	I ....
When I get difficult news about our child	I ....
When I have to attend a meeting/ appointment about our child	I ....
When I'm frustrated	I ....

OTHER MEMBERS OF THE FAMILY

It is important too to acknowledge that other members of the family will have feelings about your child's additional need. They may also find the diagram on page 43 interesting to look at in order to cope with their difficult feelings. Grandparents in particular may find talking about their feelings helpful as they are not just feeling emotions relating to their grandchild but also relating to their own child. On the other hand, some members of the older generation are uncomfortable talking about their feelings, and may try to keep a 'stiff upper lip', which can leave important things unsaid. Use the 'emotions' diagram as a tool to help them start talking.

ACKNOWLEDGEMENT VERSUS ACCEPTANCE

Parents report that professionals often talk about families 'accepting' that their child has an additional need. This term in itself provokes strong reactions. The dictionary definition of 'accept' is 'to consent to receive or undertake something offered'. The majority of parents of children with disabilities will not feel that they have been able to consent to a diagnosis, more that it is something given to them whether they want it or not. It might be more appropriate for you to think about acknowledging or adjusting to the diagnosis your child has been given, or even to their lack of diagnosis. These terms recognise that parenting a child with an additional need is an ongoing process. The process of acknowledging and adjusting can take time, and you and your partner are likely to adjust at different rates. You each may find different aspects of the diagnosis hard to accept.

Sue's son Charles is 17 and has a diagnosis of Asperger's syndrome.

> I can accept the diagnosis, particularly as Charles, who is very articulate, has said that he wouldn't want not to have Asperger's. He feels that it is an important part of his identity.
>
> Sue

Suzi highlighted that the acknowledgement that your child has additional needs is an ongoing process.

> We think we accept that our son is autistic. Well, we accept it at the moment, but as he grows older and the gap widens between him and his peers I suspect that we'll keep going through the process of trying to come to terms with his condition.
>
> Suzi

Tina's twin daughters have cerebral palsy. Both use wheelchairs and need adult help to meet their basic needs.

> You never 'accept' as you don't want it that way — you just deal with it.
>
> Tina

RECEIVING A DIAGNOSIS AND DEALING WITH IT TOGETHER

The parents who contributed to this book have lots of advice to share on the subject of receiving a diagnosis. Their experiences may help to make your journey less painful.

At the time of diagnosis you take little in and then questions flood your brain for days afterwards. Write these feelings and questions down to share at the next appointment.

Jean

Buy a notepad for yourself and your partner to write down thoughts as they come into your head, questions that you would like answering. Sharing these notes can help to open up the channels of communication and to understand what each of you as a couple are concerned about.

The message to professionals is clear, as one parent explains, 'The news should be conveyed empathically and professionals should actively offer parental support.'

Julie says that her family felt abandoned by the professionals after the initial diagnosis. A social worker allocated to the family described how he could be involved and told them to contact him if required.

We were naïve and didn't want to bother him. If you are struggling, don't be afraid to ask for help.

Julie

At your appointment ask who can support your family emotionally following the diagnosis.

Allowing yourself to grieve is important.

You have lost something: the future you planned when you first found out that you were pregnant just changed in the time it took someone to say 'disabled' or 'special needs'.

Suzi

Information has proved to be key for many of the parents whom we talked to.

It is important to try to inform yourself as much as possible, not just medically but try to find out about support groups either locally or online. It really helps to talk to other parents in a similar situation.

Nicola

The organisation Contact a Family (see page 187 for contact details) can put you in touch with other parents. Sometimes it helps to talk to somebody who has been through a similar situation. Scope's Face 2 Face (see page 187) befriending service trains parents of disabled children to offer emotional support to other parents.

Many parents talked about the joy of having their child.

Enjoy your baby/child for who they are and that first and foremost. The diagnosis is just a part of who they are, not only what they are.

Vicky

IN SUMMARY

From the first moment you suspect something isn't quite right to the time when you get a diagnosis for your child, you can feel as though you are on an emotional rollercoaster. The ride doesn't stop once you have got a name for your child's condition: in many ways this is just the start. You and your partner are likely to have very different feelings at different times. Each of you needs to take time to identify your own feelings and coping strategies. You then also need to make time to share your emotions, however painful it feels. By taking time out to listen and be heard, you can keep your relationship growing and build a powerful partnership.

3

Impact on everyday life

In this chapter

Having a child with an additional need will impact greatly on your daily life. As well as your immediate family, other members of your family such as your parents will be affected by your child's disability. It may also shape your friendships and your ability to socialise. Being a parent is challenging anyway but when your child has an additional need your parenting skills can be tested to the limit, particularly when your sleep may be disturbed on a regular basis and you have challenging behaviour to deal with. This chapter looks at the issues that you may face as a family. Other parents share their stories about how they survived and triumphed in similar situations too.

HAVING MORE CHILDREN

If you only have one child you may find yourselves considering making an addition to your family. When your child has additional needs, however, this decision can be harder. Some parents we spoke to had decided that they were only just coping with their child's needs and could not possibly consider bringing another child into the world, leaving them feeling a sense of longing for the family that they would never have.

Other parents are afraid that there was something genetically wrong. The fear of history repeating itself and giving birth to a second child with a similar condition can be terrifying. Some parents decide that it is not fair on another child to have to live with their sibling's disability and difficulties and therefore make the choice not to have more children.

Read on to find out more about the effects of having a sibling with additional needs within the family. If you are unsure about whether to have another child, this section can help. If you have more than one child you will find useful tips from other parents on coping.

THE IMPACT ON SIBLINGS

The Every Disabled Child Matters campaign estimates that there are 770,000 disabled children in the United Kingdom. The average family size is currently 1.8 children. It can therefore be estimated that there are 616,000 siblings of disabled children in the country.

Angela has two daughters. Charlotte, 15, and Lilly, 18, who has choreo-athetoid cerebral palsy with associated learning difficulties.

> The impact on Charlotte of having a sister with a disability has been huge. She is easily embarrassed by some of the things that Lilly does, such as eating with her mouth open and the smell that accompanies her bowel disorder. We realise the added pressure that Charlotte is under. We give her plenty of opportunities to talk to us and have offered her counselling, but she says that she doesn't need it.
>
> Angela

Family services tend to be directed towards the child with the disability rather than the siblings whose needs can become secondary. This can result in feelings of jealousy and resentment towards the disabled child. Siblings may find that the amount of attention they receive from their parents is significantly reduced, particularly when parents are suffering with depression.

It is important that the impact of being a sibling of a child with an additional need is recognised. Talk openly to your other child or children. Give them a chance to say how they feel and listen to their experiences without judging.

Set time aside for your other child where they can have your full attention. This may mean that one of you has to look after one child while the other parent spends quality time with their sibling(s).

Carla Thompson runs a counselling and parenting support service in Staffordshire. Her contact details can be found on page 190.

Family counselling gives members of the family the opportunity to express their feelings and give each other support. Family members are helped with possible feelings of anger, guilt, shame, jealousy and other inter-relationship issues through these sessions.

Family counselling will also look at updating parenting skills, building confidence and very often bringing the members of the family together. A disabled child can take up so much of the parents' time and attention that other siblings may feel neglected but don't mention it because they don't like to add to their parents' stress or they simply take it for granted that their needs come second to the disabled child's.

While there may be negative feelings about being a sibling of a disabled child, it frequently has positive consequences, such as learning about caring and love. The disabled child gives out to others, enabling others to develop skills and qualities they may not otherwise have known about.

All these issues, the good and the not so good, can be discussed and explored in family therapy. I help to move the family forward so that they can help themselves, by teaching them for example how to hold weekly 'family meetings' where worries and feelings are openly discussed and where the family can look at ways of overcoming problems that occur.

Carla Thompson, counsellor and psychotherapist

If you feel that family counselling is something that you wish to consider there are a number of ways to gain more information. Carla Thompson says that some families can access the therapy through the NHS or Family Services provided by Social Care. Others may prefer to see a private family therapist. 'The number of sessions required depends upon the needs of the family,' she says, 'but most family counselling will take around eight to 10 sessions, which will probably be spread over three to six months.'

Joy explains that her daughter Maria, age 16, has cerebral palsy and challenging behaviour which has impacted on her son Robert, who is 12.

My daughter's additional needs have no doubt impacted on my son. It's been difficult to give my son individual quality time without adapting our lifestyles. Life has to be planned and cannot be impulsive.

Joy

Consider how you can make time for your other children. Are you able to ask a relative to watch your child for a couple of hours while you spend time with their sibling? Could you investigate local respite options by contacting your social care department? Or are there any local clubs that your child with an additional need could join which would benefit them socially and free up some of your time?

Using support groups

Support groups can make a difference to siblings' lives, allowing them the opportunity to meet other children who are in similar situations. Such groups allow children to have their feelings acknowledged and can reduce their feelings of isolation. Your child can learn coping strategies and identify and build support networks.

Sometimes siblings believe that they have to take on responsibility for their disabled brother or sister. John is 18 and his brother, Sam, has a diagnosis of autism and learning difficulties. John told us that he fully expects to take care of his brother when his parents are too old to take the responsibility.

I love my brother and I have to help out as the strain sometimes gets too much for my parents. He soils himself and I change him. It's not really how I want to spend my time but we all muck in. I know one day my parents won't be able to give Sam the level of care that he requires, then I suppose it will become my duty.

John

Siblings of disabled children benefit from meeting other siblings and having the opportunity to share their experiences of family life. Sibling groups give them the opportunity to do this by combining recreational and discussion-based activities. Groups often run weekly for eight to 10 consecutive weeks. During this time siblings have a break from home life, make new friends, learn about disability, and test out strategies for coping with difficult issues such as worry or being teased about their family.

One child who attended a sibling group says, 'People here at the sibling group were really helpful. They listened to our problems and gave us ideas on how to deal with them.'

After attending a sibling group siblings feel less isolated, they talk more to parents about their concerns, they cope better with challenging situations and they have more confidence in themselves. Many parents also report improved relationships between siblings at home.

Monica McCaffrey, director of Sibs

SIBLINGS AND THE FUTURE

It is important that as a family you do discuss the future. It is not fair to expect siblings to take on the care of their brother or sister and it is often not necessary if appropriate plans are put into place. Organisations such as Sibs (see page 188 for contact details) can offer advice on planning for the future. Many couples feel that they need help with parenting a sibling. The Sibs helpline takes calls from parents requesting help with a wide variety of issues such as helping siblings to deal with worry, maintaining family relationships and how to explain about disability to other children. So if you do need support you are certainly not alone.

HAVING AN ONLY CHILD

If you make the decision not to have another child you can be left with further feelings of loss and grief. You may have always dreamt of having several children and now it may feel as though this dream has been shattered. It is important that you speak to your partner about your feelings of loss openly and honestly.

You may wish to talk to a counsellor about your feelings if you are finding them difficult to come to terms with. Think about whether you have hidden feelings of resentment that you will never have more children. You may have built up a subconscious picture of 'normal' family life with two or more children, and need help to move on to accept your new reality. Getting help to explore these feelings is important: you can otherwise find your hidden feelings turn into anger with your partner or child.

SUPPORT NETWORKS

Support from family members

The extended family can be a tremendous support mechanism when you have a child with a disability. Your family can also sometimes place a terrific strain on you.

> I can't cope with emotionally propping up my mother as well as trying to function. She phones me constantly if she knows that we have had a hospital appointment, wanting to know what was said. I understand that she loves Jake and is concerned but sometimes I just do not want to keep talking about it and going through 'why' it had to happen to Jake.
>
> Laura, whose son has cerebral palsy as a result of birth trauma

It may be useful to unplug the phone for a few hours until you feel that you are ready to speak to people. Explain in advance that you have things to do and won't be able to speak with them until later in the day.

> Every one of our family has a cure for our child's autism. Or they blame us for bad parenting, bad diet or something else. No doubt they mean well so I smile and say I'll look into the cure.
>
> Suzi

Although it is not possible for everyone, having family members who are willing to look after your child eases pressure and allows parents some much-needed leisure time.

Some people with disabled children have incredibly supportive families, which removes the need to use respite care.

Angela

Talk through practical ideas with your partner to help to reduce your stress levels. Working things out as a couple can reduce stress and help you share the job of keeping the family informed.

Ideas to help inform the family:

- Could your partner take responsibility for feeding back information to their side of the family?

- Could you email family members with updates from appointments so that you do not have to relive it several times over?

- More and more parents are using a blog to share information with the family. Blogs are free online journals. Using a password will keep the information more private if you want to limit access to your family only.

It is important that you explain to your families how challenging life can be and that while you appreciate their support at times you feel unable to answer their questions as you are dealing with your own difficult feelings.

Support from friends

Becoming a parent can put a strain on friendships. New parents find that they can be seriously lacking in social time. When your child has additional needs it can be harder to maintain friendships, particularly as many friends are unable to empathise with your situation.

> I'm a single parent of two children with special needs so I don't get to go out much. [Friends] really don't understand my situation. One friend even asked when they'd get better.
>
> Tracey

Other parents have found that they have lost contact with friends as a direct result of their child's disability.

> I lost lots of friends when my son was obviously not 'normal'. I felt isolated as he had to go to a special needs school. It left me feeling like a leper and most of my friends just stopped seeing us as he was difficult to be around.
>
> Sally

Suzi has noticed that some of her friends find it difficult to know what to speak to her son about, so she makes sure she gives them prompts. This is good advice. Sometimes friends may just need pointing in the right direction about how to interact with your child.

Most of our friends just don't have a clue. When I comment on my son's lack of short-term memory, for example, which is a major problem, they say 'Oh yes, mine's just the same. Boys, eh?' You just can't explain that this is on such a different scale, they simply don't get it and it leaves you feeling patronised and frustrated.

Roberta

Other couples talked about their friends being incredibly supportive. Sue's son Charles has been funded for a one-year course by one of their friends.

We are not as reliable due to Luke's needs. If we make arrangements to go out we often have to cancel at the last minute, but our friends are very good about it. They have been very supportive and continued to visit, listen and share the tough times. They have also helped us to put things into perspective when things have been really tough. They all deserve a great big thank you.

Sharon

Angela says that most of her friends don't understand, but she recently confided her worries to a couple. 'Both were shocked as they thought I was coping well,' she says.

I have one friend who has known me a very long time. She came on holiday with me and my daughter once and spent 11 days with us. She said afterward that she had never realised what it was like for me.

Anne

Sometimes it may be necessary to explain clearly to your friends the difficulties that you face and the support that you need. They may be willing to help more but genuinely do not understand what you need, or mistakenly believe you are coping well.

Julie says that most of her friends have been made through her daughter.

I'm a proactive parent and am involved in various voluntary groups. I have become good personal friends with colleagues through these groups. These friends are very supportive and some are empathic, truly understanding what I'm going through.

Julie

Outside support

Lisa runs a group on Merseyside called Sundowns that supports more than 60 families in the area who have a child with Down's syndrome. (Details of the group can be found on page 188.) The group was set up in 2000 after four mums had baby girls with Down's syndrome in the same hospital within six months of each other. After developing a friendship they decided to set up the group so that other parents would not feel the same isolation that they had experienced.

> We offer families the opportunity to take part in day trips. This helps in a number of ways. First of all, families with disabled children are often suffering from financial hardship so our support group covers the full cost of the day for the whole family. Also, many families feel more comfortable taking part in trips with support from other families in the same situation. Our group also provides information and training to families so that they are kept informed about local provision and our bi-monthly newsletter helps to keep families up to date.
>
> Lisa, of Sundowns

As well as providing information, Lisa feels that Sundowns offers parents a great deal of emotional support.

> As a parent with a child who has special needs I find that being part of a support group is hugely beneficial. Support groups aren't for everyone but we encourage families to take as little or as much as they want from the charity. I think we would all agree that we have made some very close friendships with people that we would not have met had it not been for our disabled children. It is like any organisation, you meet people who you would

not choose to socialise with but you also meet people who become a very important part of your life. People you know that you can ring at any time of the day or night and moan or cry to because they understand the situation that you are in.

Lisa, of Sundowns

Support groups appear to be a great place for parents to make friends. Some parents talked about using the internet as a way of finding others to talk to and of friendships developing online.

Dads can often feel unsupported as though they have nobody to talk to about their child.

When my son was born with Down's syndrome it was as though I'd not become a father. Usually the lads from work go to the pub to wet the baby's head but nobody really knew what to say to me so Declan's birth was ignored and that really hurt.

David

Lisa says that Sundowns encourages fathers to join in with the activities.

Dads do attend and we try to make as many of our events as family-orientated as possible. The mums have wine and pizza nights and the dads have the odd curry night. We also have couples nights where we might go out for a drink or have a BBQ. Many of the dads have also formed close friendships and act as a support network for each other.

Lisa, of Sundowns

Getting help when you need it

It can be hard to find help at a time of crisis. If you are in the midst of a stressful situation you may find that you bottle up all your feelings until you have a spare moment, then have no-one to support you. John and his wife have three children and one of their sons has Down's syndrome.

I think having a child with special needs causes me to worry about the long-term future more than otherwise. When you add a full-time occupation and perhaps some part-time education on top, the responsibility and level of effort can be overwhelming. Sam was diagnosed with Down's syndrome at birth and initially it was a very difficult time because my wife was in the hospital and I was at home with the other two children. I felt pressure to stop relatives upsetting my wife. I tried to put a brave face on things and tell my wife and relatives that everything was going to be OK. This meant that I had no support at all.

On the evening of finding out my son had Down's syndrome, after my other children and my mother-in-law had gone to bed, I broke down and cried.

I was so upset and had no-one to talk to so I phoned the Samaritans. I wasn't suicidal, I just didn't have anybody to talk to and I needed to talk to someone without pretending that everything was OK. The Samaritans were great, I just cried down the phone, they were very supportive and I felt so much better. I'm so grateful for them being there for me.

John

If you need to talk to someone urgently, you can find contact details for the Samaritans at the end of the book.

HELP FOR DADS

If you are a father and feeling very alone in your situation, some organisations do have dads' support groups. It is worth asking a health worker if they know of any locally. If there aren't any groups specifically aimed at fathers you could consider attending a parent support group as a couple. Your GP's surgery is likely to be able to put you in touch with a counselling service too.

Do not feel weak for asking for help: sharing your feelings with someone outside the situation can act like a vent and help you carry on with day-to-day life.

SLEEP

Sleeping issues

Parents of children with a disability report that sleep deprivation is a major issue. Research has shown that children with a disability are far more likely to have sleep issues than other children. These can include issues such as failure to settle at night, frequent waking, bed-wetting or sleepwalking. Many mums and dads who completed our survey said that they were sleep-deprived.

It is worth mentioning at this point that sleep deprivation is a form of torture and can leave you feeling depressed, unable to cope and exhausted. When you have a baby you expect some degree of sleep loss: what you don't expect is for this to continue indefinitely. Good quality sleep is essential not only for the child but also for the parents. Sleep deprivation affects your performance, be it at school, home or work.

Sometimes it is clear to see why a child is waking; Joanne's son has cerebral palsy and wakes up constantly at night screaming in pain.

> Daniel is unable to roll over in his sleep and so gets stuck in one position at night. This can get painful for him. My husband and I now go to bed at different times to cover Daniel's night-time difficulties in shifts. Obviously this impacts on our relationship as a couple.
>
> Joanne

Joanne and her partner have found a method of coping with the sleep disturbance that works for their family. Although they are both still exhausted from the night wakings they have devised a system whereby one partner is on duty at a set time and then the other takes over. This ensures that they don't argue over whose turn it is and they both know that they are guaranteed some sleep each night.

Any night-time disturbance can have an effect on your sex life. Arabella, for example, admits she is always too tired, 'which is causing problems for us'.

See later in this chapter for more advice on this.

A number of parents told us that their children have never slept well but as they get older they amuse themselves rather than wake the adults.

Charles has never slept well, but he doesn't come into our bedroom now. Early on he did. Children are excellent forms of contraceptive.

Sue

One parent had worked with a sleep adviser and found it highly successful.

Aron has autism and never slept well. I consulted a sleep adviser and she gave us a sleep diary to keep. She asked lots of questions about his sleep and his bedroom and devised a sleep programme based on cognitive behaviour management. Within two weeks his sleep was much improved.

Parent

Ask your health visitor or GP what support is available in your area. Some local authorities have sleep practitioners who are trained to work with children with additional needs. Sleep Solutions is a charity that delivers workshops to parents around sleep issues when their child has an additional need. The workshop includes information about basic sleep hygiene. Sleep Solutions' contact details can be found on page 188.

If your sleep is regularly disrupted it would be helpful for you to keep a sleep diary. Complete the diary for a two-week period to give a clear picture of any pattern emerging. If you want to use the drug melatonin to aid sleep, doctors often want to see evidence that you have tried alternative methods.

It may be helpful to keep the diary by the bed so that you don't have to go searching for it.

Sleep Diary

	Night 1	Night 2	Night 3
Any daytime naps?			
Bedtime routine problems			
Time put to bed			
Time fell asleep			
Night wakenings – time and duration			
Time woken in morning			
Any other problems?			

	Night 4	Night 5	Night 6	Night 7
Any daytime naps?				
Bedtime routine problems				
Time put to bed				
Time fell asleep				
Night wakenings – time and duration				
Time woken in morning				
Any other problems?				

Sex and disturbed sleep

Obviously, having little sleep or continually disturbed nights takes its toll on your sex life. At times you may feel like you couldn't care less about sex, but your partner may not agree. At other times, you may be interested when your partner is too tired to care, and you can end up feeling rejected. Putting some effort into maintaining a sex life is a worthwhile way of looking after your relationship.

Firstly, remember that almost all parents and couples in long-term relationships go through periods where they have less sex. Even if you don't feel like 'doing the deed', make time to be close to each other.

Make time for romance

Book regular nights in where you share a favourite meal or drink. Take a glass of wine or some chocolate to bed to share, and remember to turn in sufficiently early so that you don't fall asleep instantly. If you don't feel like sex, talk about this and make a point of spending time kissing and cuddling.

Many of the parents we spoke to reported that their sex life had been affected. Some felt that it was a natural part of parenthood and that their child's additional needs had not had an impact. Others, however, could identify that the stress of parenting their disabled child had impacted directly on life in the bedroom.

A number of parents reported that they were taking anti-depressants and that this affected their libido, meaning that sex was the last thing on their minds. Others reported that they were simply too tired and viewed bed as the place to sleep.

Julie is now divorced but says that when she was married her sex life was seriously affected.

> We had twins, both with cerebral palsy, and were just too tired from juggling everything to have a sex life. Initially I was scared too that I'd get pregnant and the same thing would happen again.
>
> Julie

You may speak to your GP who can arrange for genetic counselling to investigate whether there is a risk of further pregnancies resulting in the child having the same diagnosis.

DEALING WITH CHALLENGING BEHAVIOUR

A number of parents talk about the stress of having to deal with challenging behaviour from their child. One of the major stresses seems to be the reaction of others, particularly when out and about in public. Couples sometimes deal with the behaviour in different ways, which can cause arguments.

Sharon says that her son, who is three years old, is just starting to demonstrate some challenging behaviour. Having worked in residential care for a number of years she is aware of the benefit of giving a child firm boundaries. She also believes in being consistent.

My husband isn't always great at being consistent and does give in sometimes. This can cause friction as it is a big no-no as far as I'm concerned.

Sharon

It is important that parents give their child consistent messages when it comes to behaviour. You could try sitting down together and discussing the following points:

- What behaviours does your child demonstrate that you find unacceptable?

- How do you intend to deal with these behaviours?

- What sanctions will you use? (Examples are time out or loss of leisure time.)

- What rewards will you offer your child for positive behaviour?

- What do you find most difficult to cope with about your child's behaviour?

VISUAL TIMETABLES

Many parents told us that even simple activities like getting ready for school or a trip to the supermarket could be a stressful event when their child has a special need. A visual timetable is a tool that can help your child know what will happen next and adapt to the change. It can also lessen stress in your relationship as you and your partner are both clear about your child's routine.

Even though we try to stick to a routine and do the same thing each morning, James finds getting ready for school challenging. I know that in school he uses a visual timetable so decided to explore whether using one at home may be useful. I spoke to his teacher to find out what kind of visual aids they use and made him something similar to use at home. It covers the key events such as getting up, brushing his teeth, getting washed, eating breakfast and getting dressed. Since we introduced the timetable, mornings have been far less stressful for us all.

Bridget

Starting the day on a positive note is essential to maintaining a good relationship between parents.

A visual timetable shows a child what will happen during each section of the day in a visual way. It can be made using real objects such as a cereal packet to represent breakfast time or a real toothbrush to show that it is time to clean teeth. Symbols can also be used. If your child is a Makaton user then you may wish to use Makaton symbols, or pictures or photographs can represent key events. The timetable can be either horizontal or vertical and a strip of sticky-backed Velcro runs down the back of it. Small pictures, photographs or symbols are stuck on the timetable with Velcro to represent different activities. Once each activity is completed the child can remove them and place them in a box.

If you are using a visual timetable for the first time you may wish to begin with fewer pictures, depending on your child's ability. Make sure you stick the timetable where it is accessible to your child. The fridge or a door can be a good place. Get down to your child's height and make sure they can see the pictures and reach the chart.

The positives about using such a timetable are that they can give your child a visual clue about the structure of the day. It promotes independence, encouraging your child to look at the timetable so that they can see what activity needs to be carried out next. If your child gets anxious a timetable can reduce their anxiety as they can see exactly what is about to happen next, which in turn increases their confidence.

At first, you may need to teach your child what each part of their timetable represents, so hand them the card and say, 'This means it is time to get dressed'. Children with learning difficulties can benefit from visual timetables as it helps them to remember what needs to be done next.

It is recommended that you trial the timetable for at least a month to assess whether it is a valuable tool for your family and your child. It may take your child this long to start to understand how it works and to respond to it.

If the timetable does work then you could consider other times of the day when you may use one. For example, if a trip to the supermarket is stressful you may consider developing a timetable to prepare your child. You may include getting ready to go out, the trip to the supermarket, choosing the food, going through the checkout, packing the bags and the return journey home.

SUPPORTING EACH OTHER THROUGH CHALLENGING BEHAVIOUR

Stella tells us that her daughter's behaviour can be challenging in public so she too recognises the need for consistency and communicates regularly with her ex-husband in order to offer support and advice.

> I discuss experiences with my ex-husband and we swap strategies. In general we are supportive of each other and have a good working relationship.
>
> Stella

Swapping stories reassures each parent that outbursts don't just happen when the child is with them. It also offers you the opportunity to talk about how the situation made you feel and what you could do differently next time.

Some parents carry small cards with them that state that their child is not naughty, they have a special need. If they see that an audience is gathering, they simply hand out the card so that they do not feel the need to explain themselves.

> I've not accepted a diagnosis of autism for my child, but I know that he is autistic. Sometimes his behaviour can be very bizarre and it is OK in the house but when we are in public I feel embarrassed. I then feel guilty about feeling embarrassed about my own child. Sometimes I think it would just be easier to accept the

diagnosis and then at least I've got a reason for his behaviour. My partner copes with it better than I do and just tells people, 'He doesn't like loud noises, and he'll be OK in a minute'. I wish I could do that.

Pamela

Sarah is mother to Michael, aged 11, who has Asperger's syndrome. Her husband Matt died 18 months ago. She tells us that Michael's behaviour can be difficult to manage.

When Matt was alive we used to help each other laugh at it. It's easy to take life too seriously now when things are bad.

Sarah

Humour seems to play an essential part in coping with difficult situations. One parent told us that it is a coping strategy that he uses a lot but sometimes he gets misconstrued as being unkind or inappropriate.

Behaviour difficulties can be extremely challenging to cope with. It is essential that you keep communicating as a couple and work in partnership in order to deal with them in a consistent manner.

Children respond best to clear, firm boundaries. If you find that you cannot agree on the best way to handle behaviour, seek advice from an outside agency. You could ask school how they deal with the behaviour and identify strategies that could work for you at home. If your child is pre-school age you could ask the health visitor for advice. Whatever you choose to do remember that you can reach common ground if you keep speaking and hearing what each of you is saying. Negotiation is key.

How Victoria did it

Victoria Ballard has a son with cerebral palsy and she set up a business manufacturing reward charts. Here she shares here experience around positive behaviour management.

The degree of each child's demands can vary so much, particularly for those children with special needs. So my best advice to any parent is to focus on the positives and don't forget to give praise where praise is due. It can be easy with the pressures of modern life to focus on the negatives, 'Don't do this, don't do that'. So often when a child does do something good or has made a conscious effort to do something it can go unremarked. Children love to know when they do well and this will help work out right from wrong.

When talking to a child in the instance of reprimanding or praising, it is good to physically get down to their level. Also, don't dwell on a subject. If a child has had a telling-off make it short, to the point, and give them an explanation of why what they have done is wrong. Then get off the subject and move on.

Nothing is instantaneous. Reward charts help bring parent and child together, they show the rewards and the progress which can be a great help and reassurance for children Our charts also give parents the flexibility to tailor their child's individual needs, which helps get to the core of an issue. But as I always say, charts don't work on their own and parent involvement is imperative.

Nobody can prepare someone for parenthood and its extremes — the good times are amazing, the not so good times are very hard work. Hopefully, over time though, parents engaging with their children will help the good times predominate.

Victoria Ballard, founder, The Victoria Chart Company Ltd

More can be read about Victoria's business in Chapter 9. For information about Victoria's charts see the useful contacts section on page 191.

THE PHYSICAL CHALLENGE

If your child has a physical disability this can put a strain on you physically as well as mentally. Lynn is a single mum and her daughter Chelsea uses a wheelchair.

I have constant backache from manhandling Chelsea. I do have equipment such as hoists which help, but I still have to physically move her to dry her and dress her once she has been hoisted from the bath.

Lynn

Mention the difficulties that you are finding to your child's consultant. They may be able to refer you to other services which can offer advice on manual handling techniques. If you have a partner, talk to them about the times of the day that are particularly hard for you.

Could your partner adjust their hours slightly so that both of you are around at particularly demanding times of the day? Going in early and coming home early is just one example of flexible working.

As the parent of a child with an additional need you have a right to request flexible working.

You could also request a condensed week, where you work four 10-hour days instead of five shorter days, or term-time working, or annualised hours where you work more at some times of the year than others. See Family Friendly Working (Antonia Chitty, White Ladder Press 2008) and www.familyfriendlyworking.co.uk for more examples and ideas.

IN SUMMARY

Daily life can be hard when your child has an additional need. It can impact not only on your relationship but on your relationship with your other children, extended family members and friends. It is important that you keep talking as a couple, identifying what is causing you stress and discuss how you can work together to improve the situation. Also, don't forget to celebrate the good things, the achievements and reflect on how well you are doing as a family. See Chapter 9 for more about celebrating your child. Remember to ask family and friends for help but be specific in what you are asking for. If you need some time for you as a couple, ask specifically if they will look after your child for a certain length of time rather than hinting that a night out would be good. Share with them how you are feeling and share your feelings with each other.

4

Additional pressures

In this chapter

- Money
- Education
- Holidays
- Work
- Housing difficulties
- The future
- More sources of help

We have already explored how becoming parents can change the dynamics of your relationship. When your child has a special need there are additional pressures. Do you worry about the future for your child? Have you got concerns about making ends meet, adapting your home and keeping up with the demands of work? Is it proving difficult to find the right educational setting for your child? All these pressures take their toll on your relationship.

In this chapter we explore the issues that couples may face and give suggestions which can help to improve the situation and at the same time strengthen your relationship as a couple.

MONEY

Couples who have a child with a disability are at higher risk of having financial difficulties. The cost associated with having a child with an additional need is higher than with other children. You can find yourself paying out to buy specialist equipment. Then there is the cost of travel for frequent hospital visits, perhaps to specialist hospitals some distance away. And childcare costs can be higher too.

Leona says that sometimes it is things that you don't consider that cost money. Her son Adam 'bum-shuffled' for a long time as he was unable to stand and so wore out many pairs of trousers.

Leona and her partner also found that frequent hospital visits cost them a lot in petrol and in food for themselves.

> We have to buy lots of clothes due to soiling. On top of this all specialist equipment is ridiculously expensive. We have had to buy three wheelchairs

over the years. Car seats cost about three times more than regular seats. We've had to buy larger cars to accommodate all of our daughter's equipment.

Angela

Many families are entitled to benefits and tax credits that they fail to claim.

The charity Contact a Family has a helpline that you can call for a benefit check. They will be able to advise you of anything that you are missing out on. Their contact details appear on page 187. You can also go to your local Jobcentre Plus for advice on benefits. Make a point of fitting this in: just a few pounds extra each week can make the difference between debt and solvency.

Money is one of the biggest causes of stress in a relationship. You may feel that you are stuck at home with a tiny budget to stretch across all the family needs and no scope for getting out to earn more. Or you may be stuck in a job because your income is essential to meet your family's bills.

Getting as much financial help as is available can be a key way to take the pressure off both of you. It will help you look after your child's needs and reduce the stress on your relationship.

If finances are a problem, sit down together and look at other ways that you could increase your income. Ideas might include using auction websites or car boot sales to generate some cash. You could take in a lodger if you have space in your home. If you are the main carer and have a little spare time in the day, think about the skills or interests that you have and consider using them to work from home. If you have typing skills you could market yourself as a virtual assistant to local businesses. You may be able to offer ironing services. If you do decide to become self-employed you must register with the Inland Revenue within three months of beginning to trade.

Debt

If you feel that you have lost control of your finances it would be useful for you to sit down together and make a list of exactly what you owe and to whom. Highlight priorities such as rent or mortgage and utility bills. See if you can switch debts with higher interest rates to a lower rate and try to pay off as much as possible to clear the debts.

It is helpful if you can speak to your creditors about your difficulties. Your local Citizens Advice Bureau can help you to work out a debt management plan.

Make a plan

You will feel more in control if you can work out a scheme with your creditors to pay back a small, affordable amount each month than if you are continually borrowing from one source to pay another. Addressing debt issues may seem difficult, but can help you get on as a couple instead of fighting over who has spent the money that should have gone to pay a bill.

EDUCATION

When your child has an additional need their education can cause additional concerns. During our research for this book many parents talked about how they felt that they had to fight to get their child's individual needs met. This in turn takes its toll on the parents' relationship and places it under further stress.

When your child has an additional need it can be difficult initially to send them to nursery or pre-school. Vicky shares her feelings about her 20-month-old daughter who has Down's syndrome.

> I am not keen to send Bethan to nursery where she may be left to get on with it as she needs so much time compared with other children. This is becoming more so now that she is at an age when most children are walking and becoming independent and she isn't.
>
> Vicky

If you are concerned about your child starting school contact your local authority's special educational needs department to find out about specialist provision in your area. Many children are now educated in mainstream schools but it is helpful to know what else is on offer. The portage service is a home visiting service for pre-school children with additional needs. More information about this service can be found on page 197.

Lack of funding to meet children's needs seemed to be a recurrent issue for the parents we spoke to. Joanne's son is 11 and attends a mainstream school.

The support that our son needed was just not available in school. As a result we have spent thousands of pounds to send him to a centre run by the Dyslexia Institute. Obviously in order to afford this we have had to forgo things such as days out and holidays, yet we recognise the importance of this support.

Joanne

Angela also identified that lack of resources for her daughter has caused problems.

I have found it hard realising that so-called professionals such as teachers don't always know what is best for your child. I now question their motives knowing that some of the information given is reliant on constraints placed upon them by budgets and staffing. We have to be our daughter's advocate for so many things. Education has been difficult as there is no provision for children like our daughter — special schools are too restrictive and mainstream schools not specialist enough.

It is my greatest regret that we have failed her in her education and I wish we had enough money to use private education for her and be even more demanding of the state. School complain about our inadequacies but when we ask them for support none is available.

Angela

Sharing your concerns

When you have concerns about your child's education it is important to share them. At first you may find that voicing them informally to staff at the school is sufficient in order for them to address them. If you have concerns about your child's education sit down as a couple and identify what these are and what changes you would like to see. You may find completing the form below a helpful exercise.

Example:

Problem	Consequences	What can be done to resolve this
Jake comes home soiled	He is uncomfortable and sore	Please can he be changed at 3pm
Jake is not eating his lunch	He is hungry mid-afternoon	Verbal prompting from staff to eat More time for him to eat

Problem	Consequences	What can be done to resolve this

Once you have identified the problem and some possible solutions it is worth speaking to your child's class teacher. They too may have suggestions for how to resolve the issue. The SENCO (special educational needs co-ordinator) would also be a useful member of staff to highlight your concerns to. If informally discussing the problems does not help, ask for a multi-disciplinary meeting. Key professionals who are involved with your child could be invited in order to develop strategies to address the issues.

Formal complaints

If you feel that the issue is not being resolved or is a serious one, you should make your concerns known to the school in writing. Outline what is causing you concern and how you would hope that the school would resolve this. Copying in the chair of the governors is useful. And keep all correspondence in a file so that you have evidence of the dialogue that has been exchanged.

The Parent Partnership Service

This service can provide valuable support. It actively works with parents, schools, local authorities and service providers to ensure that all children, young people and their families have a positive educational experience. It is designed to ensure that parents and carers of children with additional needs have access to information and guidance on matters relating to special educational needs. This can help you as parents to make informed decisions about your child's education. It is a confidential and impartial service for families with children from birth to 19 years. Contact the special educational needs department of your local authority to find out about the service in your area.

Transition

When children move to different schools it is always a difficult time for parents and the child.

When my son moved from Foundation Stage 1 to a new school it was all dealt with very efficiently. A transition plan was put into place so that the staff knew all about his needs. For example, he will only drink from a red cup. It is this sort of detail that is key for him to be able to settle well in a setting.

Now he is due to move from Year 6 into secondary school and I'm gravely concerned. I know that adaptations will need to be made to the building as he has a physical disability. I also realise that staff will need to be trained in moving and handling techniques. He can't just arrive on the first day without this support being put into place. I've mentioned my concerns to the school that he will be moving to but nobody seems to have any sense of urgency.

What I've now done is requested a meeting with his new head of year and with his current class teacher so that I can outline his needs. I don't think I should have to be so proactive to be honest. I'd expect the professionals to be thinking ahead, but they aren't.

Martin

Getting a good transition package in place for your child is vital to support them when moving settings. Ask your child's current school how they intend to support the move at least six months before it is due to happen. It is good practice to have a meeting with representatives of both schools present and for your child to visit the new school. As parents, identify the times of the day that you think they find challenging and share this information with the staff. Make suggestions regarding how they should work with your child and share what motivates them.

Remember that while teachers may be the experts when it comes to education, you are the experts about your child. A smooth transition helps to relieve stress at home and on your relationship, so it is worth investing time in it.

HOLIDAYS

Couples agree that holidays are more costly if a child has an additional need. You may have to pick accommodation with specialist equipment available on site, such as hoists and disabled toileting facilities, making it impossible to get a good deal or a late break.

Hiring a private villa for holidays was the best solution, although this often works out more expensive than package holidays.

Jean

Other families have invested in a static caravan and adapted it to meet their needs.

It is important that you get a break as a couple and some quality time together. Some couples are able to leave their child with family members to enjoy a short break.

If you do not have anybody to look after your child think about approaching your social worker and see whether there are any local respite opportunities. You may feel reluctant to leave your child but the whole family can benefit from the break. Your child will be looked after in a caring environment and you can go back to your role as parent and carer feeling refreshed.

If you would prefer to go away together there are a number of purpose-built centres across the country that provide holidays for families and children with additional needs. These offer reduced-price breaks and contact details can be found on page 191.

Some local authorities offer families grants for holidays. These are often small but it is worth asking your social worker for details.

Family fund

The government-funded charity Family Fund may offer grants to families who have a child age 15 or under with a severe disability. Contact details can be found on page 192. Some charities offer funding for holidays. Look up the charities that are associated with your child's condition to see if they have any funding on offer.

WORK

Many couples plan on having two incomes after the mother's maternity leave is over. When a child is born with additional needs this plan may have to change, with one parent taking on the role of full-time carer.

> I had to stop working outside the home as childcare was impossible. I moved to working in the evenings when my husband was around to look after the children, but he couldn't cope. I ended up leaving work and have now set up my own business.
>
> Nicola, who runs an online store selling heirlooms and high-quality toys at www.ninnynoodlenoo.co.uk

Dave has negotiated more flexible working patterns with his employers so that he can be at home to support his wife.

> I asked to work from home and this has really helped me and Marie as a couple. She appreciates having some adult conversation throughout the day and I appreciate the flexibility of being able to help her out if things are tough.
>
> Dave

If you are in employment it is worth approaching your employers to see if they can offer you any flexible working opportunities. Parents of children with additional needs up to the age of 18 are entitled to ask for flexible working. This may mean getting in later, so you can help get your child up, or leaving early some days. There are lots of other options for flexible work.

If one partner is out at work, the person at home caring for a child may feel a loss of identity.

I used to have a career and enjoyed going to work. Now I'm stuck in the house most of the time and I resent this. I don't work because our daughter needs me at home to care for her. It is impossible to get childcare and I can't find a job that fits in around school hours.

Carole

If you can relate to feeling a loss of identity it may be worth exploring local voluntary opportunities. This can give you a sense of purpose outside of the home while developing skills for the future. Speak to your partner about how you are feeling. It is important for a healthy relationship that your self-esteem is intact. When you have things to look forward to and enjoy your confidence will increase and this will impact positively on your relationship as a couple.

I am now a full-time carer and for most of my child's life I've been a single mum. I have tried to work part-time but this has been unsuccessful due to childcare restrictions and the fact it isn't lucrative. I now do a lot of voluntary and community sector unpaid work to maintain my skills and to give me a role other than a carer.

Suzanne

HOUSING DIFFICULTIES

Problems with housing can put a strain on you and your partner. Inadequate, insufficient or ill-designed space can make day-to-day living a physical strain. Problems with sleeping arrangements can make it hard to get time together as a couple too. Some families have needed to have their home adapted or have moved house altogether in order to meet their child's physical needs. Moving puts additional strain on your relationships and finances, but can be necessary.

We had to move house in the end as our son is a wheelchair user and just couldn't access our home. Our local housing authority helped us to find a home that was more suitable for his needs and helped us to adapt it as necessary. It was a difficult decision for both me and my wife to leave our old home but we have found that we have all had a much better quality of life since we made the move.

John

If your house isn't meeting the needs of your family ask your local authority if they can carry out an assessment. They may be able to fund work that will make the house more accessible. They will not fund work that has already been started or has been completed.

THE FUTURE

It is natural to worry about the future, and the couples we spoke to for this book told us that they do worry. Their worries include:

- Who will care for their child?

- Financial issues.

- Their relationship.

Many couples find that writing a will can help to alleviate some of the stress that they feel when thinking about their child's future. Mencap has produced a guide for parents that provides useful information about writing a will and setting up a trust fund. The charity's contact details can be found on page 188 and it can also provide you with a list of solicitors.

If you are worried about an issue, talk to your partner. Set aside a time when you are both feeling calm and explain that you have something that has been bothering you that you would like to share with them. Ask your partner for their views on the problem and if they can see a way forward. Taking positive action usually helps you to feel better rather than just worrying.

MORE SOURCES OF HELP

With all these additional pressures, you can feel as if you are at the end of your tether. Stress about money, work, school and never getting a break mounts up and takes its toll on every relationship. One source of help is a family support worker.

Family support workers are practitioners who are committed to working with children and families. They work with parents and carers to help them to support their own families. It can be helpful to have a family support worker as they can assess the situation and consider what resources your family and the community have between them to address the issues and also identify any additional support that is required. Your local Sure Start children's centre may be able to provide you with details of family support workers if your child is under five years old.

Some charities also have family support workers so it may be worth contacting a charity associated with your child's condition in order to find out if they have a service that you could access.

Home-Start is a national charity with 337 schemes across the country. A family can self-refer as long as there is one child in the household who is under five years old. One of Home-Start's aims is to put the fun back into family life, and to do this it helps to increase the independence and confidence of families. The service uses trained volunteers who have parenting experience themselves and who can take the time to listen to your difficulties and offer practical support. A volunteer will visit you at home for a couple of hours once or twice a week.

IN SUMMARY

Looking after your relationship as a couple can be difficult when you have additional pressures in your lives. Acknowledge that school, housing, money and work can be causes of stress. Talk to your partner about what you might do if problems occur. By discussing how you will sort problems out before they occur you will be better equipped as a couple to deal with them. Be prepared by finding out about as many sources of grants and benefits as you can. Even if you don't need it now, it may be helpful at a time of need. And together you can plan for the future.

5

Communication is the key

In this chapter

- Poor communication
- Understanding the opposite sex
- Developing listening skills
- Don't play the blame game
- Saying what you mean
- What to do when you can't agree
- Intimacy
- Talking to others
- Counselling
- Domestic violence

Do you find that you keep having the same arguments? Has some of the intimacy disappeared from your relationship? Are you considering counselling? It is vital for all couples to communicate effectively in order to keep the relationship healthy. If you have a child with an additional need you may find that you have more issues facing you and less time to communicate with each other.

In this chapter we focus on how to resolve disagreements. You will find tips on how to negotiate with your partner in a positive way. We will look at how people communicate differently and how to develop your communication skills. Intimacy can be affected when your child has a special need and we will explore simple tips in order to relight the spark between you and your partner. We will also explore who can help if your relationship has hit a crisis.

POOR COMMUNICATION

When couples aren't communicating effectively with each other their relationship can break down. Poor communication can happen because either effective listening is not taking place or because issues are not being discussed.

The ability to talk and listen to each other is probably the most important skill to develop in a relationship in order to keep it healthy.

UNDERSTANDING THE OPPOSITE SEX

In general, men and women tend to communicate for different purposes but it is important to recognise that we are all individuals and therefore the traits that are described here may not apply to everyone. This section is not about changing the way your partner communicates but about understanding the differences more clearly.

Women usually tend to think more in terms of emotions and may communicate to express how they are feeling. For example, Helen says, 'I'm really unhappy about the way today's appointment went.' Men are more likely to communicate in order to provide solutions. So Helen's partner Mark's response may be, 'Well, we'll write a letter to the school and complain.'

While Mark's suggestion is a very practical thing to do and will move the situation forward, Helen's emotional distress has not been acknowledged. This could lead her to feel frustrated that she hasn't had the chance to explore her feelings and in turn lead to an argument as Mark will feel that he has supported her by providing a solution.

If you see this happening in your relationship, listen to what your partner is saying and think of ways to acknowledge their feelings before offering a solution. When Helen says, 'I'm really unhappy about the way today's appointment went.' Mark could respond with, 'I agree. It left us both feeling frustrated and unhappy.' Helen may then want to talk more about how she feels, before she is ready to listen to suggestions of what to do next.

It is important that you are aware of your own communication style so that you can then explain clearly to your partner what you are trying to achieve. Make an effort to focus on what you are saying and try to think about whether what you have said has met the needs of your partner.

Don't assume that your partner understands what you have been trying to say. You will be clear about what you are trying to communicate but has the message been understood? Ask your partner what they have understood and, if the main message has not been communicated, try to explain it again.

Remember that all communication styles are equal and that just because you communicate for a different purpose to your partner, yours is not the 'right' way. Respect the way that your partner communicates and accept that the difference in style can be a positive for your relationship. When we don't acknowledge differences in styles of communication we can become resentful. For example, Helen may wrongly assume that her partner Mark does not care about how she feels because he has not responded to what she said about how she felt.

DEVELOPING LISTENING SKILLS

Listening is an important skill to keep a relationship alive.

My marriage ended recently and the main reason was that my husband did not listen to me. Whenever I tried to bring up a problem he went on the defensive and tried to blame me for the difficulty. I wasn't looking to blame anybody, just to express how I felt and to be heard.

Rachel

It is vital that you and your partner both feel 'listened to' in order for your relationship to be successful. Make sure that you focus your attention on your partner and really hear what they are telling you. Turn the television off and make sure that you don't become distracted by other things. If you are very distracted explain this to your partner and suggest that you discuss things at another time when you can give them your full attention.

Things to remember

Check that you have understood what has been said. Summarise what you have heard and ask if you have received the right message. Ask about how your partner is feeling and be respectful when they talk about their emotions. Don't immediately try to 'fix' the situation by offering solutions. Spend some quality time listening to your partner to ensure that you have the full picture.

DON'T PLAY THE BLAME GAME

When you are in a difficult situation it is easy to want to find someone to blame. Often, however, there is no-one obviously at fault, which can leave you feeling the need to place blame somewhere but with no obvious solution. This can be the case if your child has had a setback.

On the other hand, if you are both unhappy and stressed about a situation it is easy to think that your partner is blaming you. When they complain about how badly things are going, you may feel criticised, even if this is not the intention. For example, if the home carer complains about how difficult it is to pay the bills, the working partner may feel blamed.

An unresolved need to blame someone is very natural, but it can lead to you becoming angry at the wrong people. It can put stress on your relationship and damage how you deal with professionals. Take some time to acknowledge when you feel angry or want to blame someone for a situation. It is good to express these feelings, but in a way that doesn't hurt those closest to you. You may want to do some physical activity, or you could find release in talking to a friend or counsellor. It is sometimes important to find someone who will help you acknowledge that you are stuck in a difficult situation, through no-one's fault.

If you feel you are being blamed for problems, talk to your partner about this at a time when both of you are calm. Simply explaining that, say, 'When you complain about struggling to pay the bills it makes me feel really bad that I don't earn more,' may make your partner think about what they say.

SAYING WHAT YOU MEAN

Sometimes it can be difficult to say openly what you want to communicate. This can be because you are struggling emotionally with the issue or because you don't want to hurt your partner. Bottling up issues can lead to health problems and relationship difficulties. It is important that you talk openly with your partner.

If you are finding it difficult to say what is troubling you, write a letter to your partner and sit with them while they read it. If you would rather speak with your partner you could write down a list of points before you talk in order to make sure that you cover everything that you want to discuss.

Make sure that when you do speak with them you do not insult them or make accusations. Communication should always be respectful.

WHAT TO DO WHEN YOU CAN'T AGREE

There are bound to be issues that you and your partner can't agree on when it comes to parenting your child. It is how you handle these issues that can impact on your relationship, either strengthening it or leading it into crisis. Most of the parents we have spoken to told us that they do have arguments relating to their child. These were about things such as how to manage behaviour and differences in opinions about medication.

Sally says that dealing with their son's behaviour caused difficulties with her relationship with her husband initially.

I probably over-compensated for our son's difficulties and my husband would be the strict one. We were operating at the extremes when it came to discipline. If my husband disciplined him then I would go and comfort him afterwards, which wasn't appropriate. We eventually learned through going to a parenting support group for Asperger's syndrome how to work together as a team. I have to say since then it has worked like a dream.

Sally

Madiha tells us how she and her husband did not have major disagreements but did have to work through differences of opinion with regard to medical matters affecting their daughter.

The doctors presented us with two options: either to have the foot of my daughter amputated or to take the path of reconstructive surgery. My husband was of the view that perhaps amputation would be a good option, whereas I thought that maybe we should give a go to reconstructive surgery and see what happens. It was by no means a major fight, it was just a difference of opinion. We made the final decision of taking the reconstructive surgery after consulting different doctors and professionals and after exploring both the options.

Madiha

When you are in a relationship it is vital to remember that you are both individuals and you will disagree at times. It is perfectly normal and healthy to have arguments but you need to ensure that you go on to meet an acceptable compromise. Rather than having an 'argument', consider together if you could have a 'negotiation'. This is a much more positive way of addressing difficulties. The following guidelines can help your 'negotiation' to remain focused and help to resolve the situation.

- Take responsibility for your feelings. Begin sentences using the word 'I' and explain how you are feeling. For example, 'I feel annoyed because I was dealing with Isabelle's tantrum when you took over.'

- Both of you should sit down as it is much easier to remain calm when seated.

- Don't use personal insults such as, 'You are so lazy.'

- Encourage each other to share feelings about the issue and listen to these respectfully without interrupting.

- Stay focused on what you are negotiating about rather than letting the negotiation drift into other areas.

- Be prepared to acknowledge your own mistakes.

- Try to put yourself in your partner's place and develop an understanding of how they feel.

- Agree a code word so that you can stop the negotiations if one of you is feeling the need to have some time alone to calm down.

- Remember you are confronting the issue, not each other.

Agreeing on how you will conduct negotiations is key to reducing conflict and confronting issues in a positive way. Try to be honest with your partner about how you are feeling and remember that having a difference of opinion and resolving it successfully will leave your relationship stronger than ever.

INTIMACY

Intimacy can mean emotional closeness as well as sexual intimacy and plays an important part in healthy relationships. Sometimes parents are too busy in their role to invest time in developing intimacy in their relationship. These tips will help you to develop intimacy.

Making time for each other

Set aside 15 minutes a day to catch up with your partner. Your own bedtime may not be a good time as you will be tired. Maybe schedule your time for after the children are in bed and before you are both exhausted.

- Ask each other about what kind of day you have had. When your partner is talking don't interrupt, listen respectfully.

- End your conversation with a hug.

I feel so guilty that I almost neglect my husband and whilst he understands that our child's needs come first, it does cause friction between us. I sometimes think how hard we've had to work to stay together but we both love each other more than ever and even if we don't have time for nights out or 'us' time, we always find the time for a hug and to say 'I love you'.

Suzi

Touch is vital for creating intimacy in a relationship. If you are exhausted and cannot even begin to think about sex, consider touch as a way of bonding with your partner. Simply holding hands can help you to feel more connected to each other. You may want to offer each other a massage or a foot rub and enjoy the intimacy that these activities bring, as well as the relaxation.

TALKING TO OTHERS

Sometimes it can help to know that you are not alone. We hope through reading the experiences of other parents in this book that you will feel less isolated. It can also help to make contact with other parents in similar situations.

I attend parents' groups and meet other parents informally. It made me realise that I'm not alone and I've gained most of my knowledge and support by networking with other parents.

Josh

Check with your child's school whether they offer any support groups in your area. You may also contact your local authority and ask if they are aware of any organisations.

Scope's Face 2 Face scheme is a national befriending service for parents of disabled children. Through the scheme you can meet another parent who has been trained by the organisation, if a local service exists. Alternatively you can be befriended through the online service and have an email buddy to share your experiences with. Talking to somebody who understands can be very helpful. Contact details for the scheme can be found on page 187.

Our befriending service provides parents with the opportunity to speak to other parents of disabled children. The befrienders can truly empathise with the parents that use the scheme as they have faced similar difficulties. Many of the parents that are befriended go on to train to become befrienders in order to support others. The service is offered free of charge and offers parents the chance to talk and to really be listened to by somebody who understands.

Lizzie Jenkins, national network manager, Face 2 Face

More can be read about the experiences of a befriender on page 170.

A new site developed by One Plus One, the UK's leading relationship organisation, is called thecoupleconnection.net. It provides online support for parents in their relationship through providing information, social networking and personal spaces. The site also includes innovative couple spaces where couples can work on their relationship together by setting goals and completing exercises, working together to make a change in their relationship.

While other social networking sites like Facebook, Bebo and MySpace are very much about broadcasting yourself to the world, this innovative site will include an area where individual parents and couples can create a private space in which to develop and strengthen their relationships.

Penny Mansfield, director, One Plus One

COUNSELLING

Many couples find counselling can help to strengthen their relationship. It is important to find a counsellor that you feel you can talk openly with. Some employers offer funded counselling for their employees or you may ask your GP for a referral, although be aware that waiting lists are usually long. Alternatively you could pay privately to see a counsellor.

Sometimes it can be difficult to seek help from a counsellor.

> It took me 15 years to ask for counselling. I felt that when my son was younger they would think I was incapable or mad and would take him away from me. It helped 100% and it should be offered to all parents who are struggling.
>
> Julie

You can attend counselling as a couple or individually. Jean went on her own.

> Counselling certainly helped. The counsellor made me believe the truth: it wasn't my fault. I'm a good person and a very good mummy. I would certainly encourage others to open up and go for counselling.
>
> Jean

During the sessions you will explore your relationship, looking at feelings, difficulties and gaining support to explore new possibilities.

Counselling can help you to view things differently and to take time out from everyday life to focus on your relationship.

DOMESTIC VIOLENCE

Sadly sometimes relationships become abusive and it is important to recognise the signs. The organisation Contact a Family surveyed 2,000 parents who have a child with an additional need and one in 10 respondents stated that the domestic violence had occurred since the birth of their child with a disability.

Abuse can manifest in different forms. There can be physical abuse which may include behaviours such as hitting, sexual abuse and punching. Emotional abuse can involve name-calling, derogatory put-downs and verbal threats. While it is usually presumed that women are the victims of domestic violence they can also be the instigators. Men who are suffering within abusive relationships may feel very isolated. While it is difficult to admit to being in an abusive relationship there are positive steps that can be taken to keep you safe. Refuges across the country provide victims with a safe place to live. On page 196 there are contact details for organisations that offer support to domestic violence sufferers.

IN SUMMARY

Throughout this chapter we have focused on positive steps that you can take to strengthen your relationship as a couple. Take some time out to discuss this chapter with your partner and be proactive in working together to identify steps that you can take to ensure your relationship goes from strength to strength.

6

Dealing with the professionals

In this chapter

- Sharing information effectively
- Attending appointments together
- An expert opinion of experts
- Early support programme
- Time pressures
- Problems with professionals

When you have a child with additional needs you often come into contact with a range of professionals. While these professionals can offer support, many parents experience difficult encounters. This chapter will look at how to communicate effectively with professionals so that you can make them aware of the stresses that you as a couple and as a family are facing. Simple tips will be included to ensure that you can work effectively as a couple with the professionals you meet. Follow these tips, as cutting out stressful meetings means less stress on you and your partner. The advice can help you and your partner work together more effectively and feel better about the outcomes you achieve from meetings too.

SHARING INFORMATION EFFECTIVELY

In order to get the best out of a relationship with a professional it is important that you and they work in partnership. While they have specialist knowledge in specific areas you are the real expert on your child. It is therefore essential that you and your partner have the chance to share your knowledge, and can do so effectively.

Sharon feels that sometimes professionals don't appreciate the complexities of life.

> Maybe if they asked 'what is a typical day like' and 'what is a bad day like' it would give them the opportunity to find out more about us as a couple. Maybe we are partly to blame for not sharing the information about what our lives entail.
>
> Sharon

ATTENDING APPOINTMENTS TOGETHER

Attending meetings about your child together is often ideal, although sometimes hard to achieve every time. If you can go together, taking time to work out a joint approach to a meeting can really help.

> As soon as possible try to get your partner to attend meetings about your child's condition and behaviour so they are informed at first hand like you. You then can avoid appearing to moan because they interact in a way your child doesn't respond to well.
>
> Arabella

You may wish to consider asking a professional if it is possible to be seen at home.

> By having professionals see children in their home environment rather than in an office they would gain a better picture of the child and how the couple are functioning.
>
> Lois

Often children and parents feel more relaxed in familiar surroundings rather than, for example, in a hospital setting. If you would like to be seen at home spend some time talking about your reasons for this and then state these to the professional.

Whether or not you will both attend, before each appointment sit down together and discuss:

- What you hope the outcome will be.

- What information you want to present at the appointment.

- Any questions that you would like addressing.

Writing these down in bullet points can help to remind you during the consultation. Don't be afraid of including the challenges that you are facing: this will help the professional to develop an understanding of how complex your life can be. Do discuss together how much you both feel emotionally able to disclose at the appointment.

> Not one expert, and we've seen many, has ever asked if we as parents are okay and coping. It's all about fixing what they think is broken, nothing about appreciating what a great part of our family our son is.
>
> Suzi

If one of you can't attend an appointment and the professional is unable to see you at a mutually convenient time, ask if you can record what is said by using a dictaphone. This can take the strain off the parent who is attending the consultation as they will not have to retell everything to their partner. It can also help your partner to feel included and to keep them fully informed.

You may also ask if your partner could have the professional's contact details. This would allow them the opportunity to have their questions answered following the consultation and to develop a relationship with the professional.

If you feel that you need support at an appointment it would be worth investigating whether there are any family support workers locally who could accompany you. You may have a trusted friend or family member who would be happy to offer you support at these times.

If you are finding it hard to cope, make a point of saying so. If you can think of something that would help, tell the professional and ask them what they would suggest.

It can be hard to admit just how close to the edge you feel some days, but it is the first step in improving the help and services your child receives.

On the other hand, if you feel that the professional is failing to see the positives regarding your family then tell them what they are. Explain to them clearly what your priorities are as a family and how you would like them to support these.

A number of parents comment that they themselves as a couple aren't aware of how complex everyday life can be until they focus on it. Jean and her husband have a seven-year-old daughter who has cerebral palsy due to clinical negligence. They say that it was only when they started to write down the daily activities that they have to complete for the medical negligence form that they realised how much stress they are under.

If you feel that it would be helpful, write down a typical day to share with the professional. A professional cannot empathise with your situation unless they are aware of the difficulties that you are facing.

Example:

Time of day	Activities	Problems	Positives
7am	Get Peter up and dressed	Physically tiring	We can both do it together
8am	Breakfast Physio exercises	Difficult to help other kids as well as Peter Hard to fit exercises in	
9am	Travel to school	Physically tiring – lifting in and out of car	
10am	Housework, washing	A lot to fit into three hours	
11am	Shopping etc		
12 noon	Collect from school	Physically tiring – lifting in and out of car Only half days as insufficient support at school	
1pm	Lunch		
2pm	Physio exercises		
3pm			
4pm	Help other kids with homework	Chaos some days!	
5pm	Tea		
6pm	Start bedtime	All takes a long time – I'm very tired by now and the kids are grumpy and tired too	Relieved when Mike gets home – a problem when he is working late.
7pm	Settle Peter		
8pm			
9pm			
Overnight	Peter wakes two or three times	Tiredness again!	

Your chart:

Time of day	Activities	Problems	Positives
7am			
8am			
9am			
10am			
11am			
12 noon			
1pm			
2pm			
3pm			
4pm			
5pm			
6pm			
7pm			
8pm			
9pm			
Overnight			

AN EXPERT OPINION OF EXPERTS

Peter Burke's academic interests span disability-related issues that impact on the whole family. His work focuses on the views of children with special needs, siblings of disabled children and the support requirements of families living with disabilities. He also has many years of experience as a parent, being father of two sons who both have cerebral palsy.

As a parent I find professionals tend to make judgemental statements. For example, after gaining a monthly respite care sitter we were told 'You have a good package of services'. At this time we had been carrying my son upstairs for 10 years. Our older son had to sleep on a camp bed in the dining room because he was too heavy to lift and we were waiting for a through-floor lift which we paid for ourselves because an assessment for a disabled facilities grant had said we were not entitled to financial help.

Another issue concerned the fact that people tend to see my job, as an academic, as somehow meaning I can articulate and gain whatever needs my family have. Not true, I am just as confused as the rest when it comes to personal matters because emotions do get in the way and objectivity is what we crave.

Peter Burke, senior lecturer in social work at Hull University

---

Updating professionals

Sometimes couples find it difficult to retell information to professionals. If you are finding it emotionally draining to keep repeating the history of your child to date you may wish to write it down. Things to include would be details about your child's needs, relevant medical history and any current concerns.

Speak to your partner about how they feel when asked to provide information about your child. If they find it easier to deal with perhaps you could agree that they answer such questions.

Be clear about supporting each other in appointments – it is fine to hold your partner's hand to show your support.

A carer's passport may be helpful. This is a folded card with your child's essential information on, such as their doctor's contact details, their date of birth, medications, and care routine. You may be able to get one from your local organisation for carers or some of the professionals you come into contact with. It can stop you having to repeat information many times and help you keep complex details of, say, medication, in one place.

EARLY SUPPORT PROGRAMME

If you have a child under five years old and live in England you could ask your practitioner whether your family can access the Early Support programme. Early Support is a government initiative that aims to achieve family-focused services for children with additional needs. The programme encourages the use of a key worker who can support the family. Information relating to your family and professionals involved is compiled in a family file that you have ownership of.

If your area is not running an Early Support programme or your child is over five years old you may still wish to look at the materials and adapt them for your own use. They are available on the website at www.earlysupport.org.uk

A Common Assessment Framework (CAF) is something else that might help you and your family. The CAF is a standardised way of assessing a child's additional needs and identifies how professionals should meet those needs in consultation with parents. Use of a CAF should help with getting more effective and co-ordinated services for you as a family and simplify the process of doing so. A form is filled in identifying your child's strengths and needs. You can ask a professional who works closely with your family and who you see on a regular basis. It could be anyone involved with the child - social worker, teacher, nursery nurse, portage worker and so on.

The CAF means that you no longer have to keep sharing your story with professionals: the information can simply be given to them to read. A CAF also identifies exactly who is involved with your family so that you don't have to constantly remember names, contact details and job titles. Professionals working with you should be able to provide you with more information about the CAF. Contact details can be found on page 195.

TIME PRESSURES

Vicky has had a more positive experience with professionals and feels that most are aware of the pressures that having a child with a special need places on the couple's relationship. But she says she isn't sure that they appreciate the pressure that can pile up through the time taken with intervention and keeping all the different medical appointments.

Be realistic

It is important to consider as a couple what is and what isn't achievable with your child. So if you are being asked to complete homework, do physiotherapy exercises, practise work from the speech and language therapist as well as bathe, feed and dress your child each evening, you need to ask for support.

Explain to each professional what you have to fit in. Ask them to think about how much it is realistic for your child to do, and make sure that they understand if you have to take care of the rest of the family too.

As a couple it is worth defining who will do what chore so that you aren't arguing about it at the time. If each of you has a defined role it will make things run far more smoothly. If you feel that what is being asked of you is not realistic you need to address this with the therapists or school as soon as possible.

I honestly had no idea that a child in my class had so many other things that needed to be done at home until his mother called me to explain why he had not done his homework. Each evening they were feeling under pressure to complete homework and for him to spend time in his standing frame as well as practise occupational therapy exercises. He often didn't get home until late anyway as he used school transport. Once it was pointed out to me I could adjust the way I worked and only send tasks home at weekends. I'd suggest that parents speak honestly to professionals. We need reminding sometimes.

Mary, a teacher

PROBLEMS WITH PROFESSIONALS

Suzanne and Mark have experienced difficulties with teaching staff at their daughter's school. Sally attends a special school for children with severe and complex learning difficulties. Suzanne and Mark are no longer together as a couple but do attend meetings and consultations together whenever possible.

Sally's teacher called a meeting at school and Mark booked time off work to attend. I booked our daughter's worker to look after her. The teacher then called the meeting off two days before it was due to happen. I found out about the cancellation via a text from Mark.

Suzanne

If you do feel the professional is not working with you effectively you could ask whether there is another member of staff who could take over your case. Ask to see the organisation's complaints policy as you may wish to lodge a formal complaint.

IN SUMMARY

Spending some time considering appointments as a couple before they occur can leave you feeling more empowered. Being clear about what you hope to achieve from the appointments can help to ensure that they are meeting your needs. Celebrate your success: tell your partner when you feel that they supported you well or put across a key point effectively. Remember that you are the expert on your child and that professionals should be partners in the processes that you are working through.

7

Coping with stress

In this chapter

We often talk about 'stress' and 'feeling stressed'. In this chapter we are going to explore exactly what stress is, the impact that it can have on our relationships and how to work towards overcoming stress.

Parenting in itself can be a stressful role and when your child has an additional need the stresses can be multiplied. It is easy to take your stress out on your partner. Throughout our research parents openly talked about feeling stressed. While it is not possible or indeed desirable to eliminate all stress from our lives, it is important to ensure that your stress levels do not get out of control as this can impact on your health as well as your relationship as a couple.

WHAT IS STRESS?

Stress is the way that your body responds to different demands and pressures placed upon it. When you feel stressed your body releases chemicals into your blood which can make you feel more energetic. This can be useful if, for example, you are feeling stressed because you are going to be attacked. The body diverts energy from digestion and other less important functions into the muscles that would allow you to fight or flee from a situation. In the 21st century, however, stress is more often due to emotional issues, and you do not achieve any sort of physical relief, so stress can cause negative effects on your body.

We almost always think about stress in association with negatives such as a marriage breakdown or a bereavement. It is interesting to note that stress can also be triggered by events that are perceived to be positive such as a wedding or even Christmas.

SYMPTOMS OF STRESS

There are a number of common symptoms of stress. Remember that we are all individuals and our bodies can react to stress in very different ways. Stress can affect our mood. It makes some people irritable, unable to concentrate or withdrawn. Stress can also affect us physically, causing headaches, or a flare-up of conditions such as mouth ulcers, eczema, asthma or poor sleep patterns.

It is important that you are aware of how stress affects you so that you can be aware of the signals that you need to look out for when monitoring your stress levels.

By exploring how stress makes you feel as individuals you can gain a greater understanding into how your partner is feeling during stressful moments. So if your partner feels irritable when they become stressed you can begin to realise that their short temper is not as a direct result of anything you have done but is a part of their stress symptoms.

If you are able to identify your own signs of stress you will also be better equipped to recognise that you are becoming stressed and to put actions into place to reduce your stress levels in future.

WAYS TO COPE WITH STRESS

Many addictions are directly linked to stress and are used as a way of attempting to manage it. For example, you may choose to 'wind down with a glass of wine' or 'relax with a cigarette'. When addictions are used in this way they offer some temporary relief from stress but they are not an effective way of managing the stress. The alcohol in a drink that initially makes you feel relaxed will also leave you feeling depressed and potentially less able to cope. The cigarette that you feel is relaxing you is in fact increasing your heart rate and blood pressure, potentially making you feel more stressed.

If you use cigarettes or alcohol to try to de-stress, look at other ways you could wind down. Sometimes having a cigarette is simply a way to step out of a stressful situation for five minutes. Could you make a cup of tea, or go into a different room and take a few deep breaths instead? Talk to your doctor if you would like help to stop smoking or cut down on drinking.

There are much better ways to deal with stress. Simply talking your situation through with someone can help, or having some 'me time', be it five hours or just five minutes.

Very simple breathing exercises could also help you feel better in a matter of minutes. Try sitting quietly with your eyes shut, count to 10 slowly while inhaling through your nose and exhaling through your mouth. Do this a few times and you will feel your body and mind relax.

Take some time as a couple to discuss stress. Answer the questions below, individually to establish how it impacts on your life, then talk about your answers together:

1. When I'm feeling stressed my body lets me know by

....

....

....

You may wish to include things like your breathing speeding up, your heart racing, or you experience stomach cramping.

2. When I'm feeling stressed I feel

....

....

....

Think about which feelings you experience, such as panic, anger, frustration.

3. When I'm feeling stressed I think

....

....

....

You may include your thoughts at the times of stress such as thinking that you are inadequate or that simple everyday tasks are unachievable.

WHAT STRESSES *YOU?*

Different people get stressed by different things. For example, some people would become very stressed by the idea of public speaking whereas other people thoroughly enjoy it. In a relationship it is important to acknowledge that you and your partner may become stressed by different aspects of parenting your child. Neither is a right or a wrong response and each partner's response is just as valid.

Pick a time when you are both feeling relaxed to talk to your partner about stress. Each write down three things in your life that make you feel stressed. Discuss what you have each written: you may be surprised by each other's answers. Then, discuss if there is any way that you can support each other to reduce the stress. For example, if one of you says that you get stressed by your child's medical appointments you could look at strategies to try to ensure that you are both present or that you discuss the appointment beforehand and make notes.

THE EFFECTS OF STRESS

Stress can have many different effects on us if it is left unaddressed. Some people may find it impossible to sleep when they are under stress while others may find that they want to sleep constantly. Stress can affect the blood cells, making you more susceptible to illness and your blood pressure can become raised. Stress can impact greatly on your relationship with your partner and minor niggles can swiftly escalate into full-blown rows. Stress hormones can lead to a loss of libido, reducing your desire to have sex. This can lead to you and your partner feeling unwanted.

THE STRESSES OF BEING A PARENT

As we have acknowledged being a parent is stressful but when your child has an additional need you may face extra pressures. Tom tells us that as soon as he received his son's diagnosis at birth his stress levels started to rise,

> At the moment I found out that he had Down's syndrome, I changed from thinking 'What a lovely son,' to 'What will happen to him when I die?'
>
> Tom

As all children and families are unique, the stresses that parents reported to us differ, but many parents did report that they found dealing with their child's challenging behaviour stressful.

> My son is extremely challenging. We both handle this differently, which causes arguments.
>
> Claire

So it is not just the behaviour that causes stress but also the different approaches that parents take that can lead to disagreements. Research has shown that challenging behaviour is best dealt with consistently. If you and your partner are finding it difficult to agree on how to handle situations it may be helpful to take time to sit down together and draw up a behaviour management plan.

It would be good to spend some time drawing up the plan when you are both feeling calm. See if you can get some care for your child while you do this, to help you both concentrate.

It is important to acknowledge that there will be disagreements and that you will both need to negotiate in order to develop a plan that you are able to work with together. If you are finding this difficult, is there a professional who could help you?

Below is an example of how to complete the plan followed by a template for you to use.

Date: *Insert the date that you draw up the plan. This helps you to monitor how your child's behaviour improves over time.*

List of behaviours causing concern:
Choose no more than three behaviours at this stage that are causing you concern. These can include things like spitting, biting, swearing, head-banging and so on.

Triggers for each of these behaviours
Sometimes it is easy to identify what triggers each behaviour. If you are able to work out what triggers them list them in this section.

Sanctions to be used
Discuss how you are going to deal with each behaviour. If your child is in education you may wish to speak with their teacher or specialist worker about techniques that they use so that you can be consistent at home. Sanctions can include things like giving a verbal warning, withdrawing eye contact, time out, distraction techniques or missing out on a favourite activity. When you fill in this section use as much information as possible. For example, you may wish to use the same words, 'John, if you hit Rachel again then you will need time out to calm down'. This signals to the child that you are working together.

Rewards to be used
Rewarding good behaviour is very important. Think about how you will reward your child when they behave as you would like them to.

You could consider using a star chart, verbal praise or a small treat. Make sure that you explain to your child what you are rewarding them for.

Review date – *review the plan in a couple of weeks to see how it has been working and amend it accordingly.*

Date

List of behaviours causing concern

....

....

....

....

....

....

Triggers for each of these behaviours

....

....

....

....

....

....

....

Sanctions to be used

....

....

....

....

....

....

....

....

Rewards to be used

....

....

....

....

....

....

....

....

Review date

....

Many parents we spoke to said that while any challenging behaviour is difficult to deal with, they feel the most stress when the behaviour takes place outside the home. Rebecca has a 16-year-old daughter who has challenging behaviour.

> I have developed a very broad back. In the past I've been the more active parent in taking our daughter out into society, but her dad is now engaging her on similar activities. I can cope with her challenging behaviour, I just become bothered when it is out in society and the general public are less than accepting of it.
>
> Rebecca

Rebecca's advice about swapping strategies is useful. It is important to realise that others may use strategies to manage your child's behaviour that work well and a little time spent sharing these techniques could come in very useful in helping you to manage a future incident.

A number of parents said that it is the stares and the tuts when out in public that really cause them stress. One strategy is to print off some business-size cards that explain that your child has an additional need and perhaps adding a website address that will explain the difficulties further. Keep the cards in a coat pocket to hand to those who stop and stare. Many parents find this a useful way of distracting onlookers so that they can concentrate on dealing with their child.

COMPLEMENTARY THERAPIES

You may wish to consider using a complementary therapy in order to manage your stress levels. Reiki, aromatherapy and homeopathy are among the many therapies available that claim to be able to help.

Sarah Holland is a therapist based in Hitchin, Hertfordshire, where she sees many clients who suffer from stress. Her contact details can be found in the useful contacts section on page 194.

> Stress, especially when it is sustained, can lead to all manner of physical symptoms including digestive problems like IBS, breathing problems, skin conditions, asthma, and much more. I have found that conditions caused by stress seem to respond particularly well to reflexology. It is estimated that 80% of all health issues are stress-related so this covers quite a few problems. Reflexology can be used safely for most medical conditions and alongside medication and treatment from your doctor.
>
> Sarah Holland, reflexologist and Emotional Freedom Techniques™ (EFT) practitioner

EFT is a method of reducing and often eliminating negative emotions such as fear, anxiety, shame and anger. The process is quick, painless and simple to learn, with results that are claimed to be real and permanent.

When stress is linked to what is happening within your family, the effect can be very deep and far reaching. Where anxiety, worry and other negative emotions have become part of you it is well worth looking into a therapy like EFT which works to eradicate the imbalances that cause these emotions, and enable us to handle situations in a rational and logical manner.

During an EFT session a client is instructed in how to tap on points on their face, upper body and hands that link to the meridians. The tapping is carried out while focusing on the problem, and therefore causing a disruption in the energy system. Clients often feel this disruption, not just as the emotion but also physically as churning in the stomach or tightness in the chest. Tapping while you are thinking about your problem will balance the body's energy so that there is no longer a disruption and you will no longer experience the negative emotion.

Sarah Holland, reflexologist and Emotional Freedom Techniques™ (EFT) practitioner

When looking for a practitioner:

- Explain the problem you are looking for help with and ask about their experience in that area.

- Check that they are insured.

- Ask if they are a member of a relevant professional body.

- Find out if they do continuing education to stay up to date.

Ask other people if they have used a therapist and found them helpful: word of mouth can be a good way to find someone suitable.

MEDICAL INTERVENTION

If you feel that your stress levels are impacting on your daily life it would be worth visiting your GP. They may be able to refer you for counselling where you would be able to speak to somebody about how you are feeling and discover ways to deal with your stress. Your GP may also be able to recommend stress management courses in your local area. If stress is causing you to feel depressed or anxious they will be able to assess whether medication is necessary.

It is possible that if it is your partner who is carrying the greater burden of caring and of stress, you may have to persuade them to take time out to have treatment or see the GP. Gently reassure them that it is quite normal to feel like this and not a sign of weakness.

Perhaps, if it is necessary, you could seek treatment together and, in turn, this would be another way you could support each other and so increase your closeness.

IN SUMMARY

Living with stress over a long period of time can be damaging to your health and relationship. If you are able to take some time out to identify the stresses in your life you will be taking a positive step towards dealing with your stress levels. Once these are identified you can discuss as a couple if there are ways of reducing the stress and how this might be achieved. Communicating with each other is the key to being supportive partners.

8

When a relationship goes wrong

In this chapter

- Break-ups
- Support networks
- Counselling
- Mediation
- Collaborative law
- Looking after the child's needs
- Communicating with your ex
- Practical matters
- Introducing a new partner

Sometimes, no matter how hard you try, relationships do come to an end. This chapter explores how to deal with a relationship breakdown, both emotionally and practically. Read tips from other parents who have been through similar situations. Explore how to communicate with your ex and look after your child's needs during a break-up. Perhaps most importantly, find out how to identify support networks and look after yourself.

Life can go on after a relationship breakdown. This chapter also looks at how to introduce a new partner to your child and the issues that this may bring.

BREAK-UPS

Parents have talked with us openly about their relationship break-ups. Some parents feel that their child's needs directly contributed to their relationship problems while others feel that it was part of a bigger problem.

> My husband and I had a very close relationship for 23 years. We had a difficult time with operations, biopsies, constant infections, a battle with school, and we felt like failures. We researched and we did our best and even better than that. I gave up my full-time career and we decided to home educate. It was the best thing that we ever did, but it was too late. My husband couldn't cope with having a child with special needs. We felt that we were constantly told that it was our fault by the school. I knew it wasn't but he couldn't accept it.

My husband has left and our relationship ended because we had no support.

Sheila

Julie's marriage broke up when her children were young. She believes that her daughter's additional needs were a factor in the divorce.

I caught my husband having an affair with a colleague from the office. I think that she began the relationship and he confided in her when he stayed for a drink after work. There were other factors too, though.

Julie

Claire has been divorced for seven years and has two children with special educational needs. She feels that her children's needs had an impact on the relationship but was not the entire reason for the marriage breakdown.

We had no time for ourselves as a couple when we were married. We both dealt with the stress of parenting in different ways and I wanted more emotional support than he could give me. My ex-husband didn't want to talk about feelings and preferred to ignore the emotional side of parenting our children.

Claire

SUPPORT NETWORKS

It is vital to have good support networks if your relationship is in trouble. A relationship breakdown is one of the most devastating things you can experience. It can leave you with a host of difficult feelings. It is important to recognise that these feelings are a normal reaction to what has happened.

I would never have believed that my marriage would have ended in divorce. When my ex asked for a divorce I had a range of emotions, from shock to disbelief and guilt to anger. The best thing I did was to establish a support network for myself and this helped to see me through the bad times. I couldn't get out to meet people as I had my son to care for so I invited friends over once he was in bed.

I also found the internet was an amazing resource for support. I joined some single parents' forums and it really helped me to realise that I wasn't alone, others were in similar situations and some were even parents of children with additional needs like me. My advice would be to seek out people who understand. They can help you so much when you are feeling down.

Joanne

Sometimes your family can provide an excellent support network. Be aware though that they are emotionally involved in your break-up. David found that although his mother wanted to offer support she had too many emotions around the break-up to be helpful.

I've always been close to my mum and when my relationship with my partner broke down it was my mum that I turned to. What I hadn't realised though was how hurt my mum was about the break-up. It's five years on now and I'm remarried and very happy with my life. Mum, however, is still resentful towards my ex. I now avoid speaking to her about the break-up as I don't find her comments useful and I don't want my daughter to hear her mother being spoken badly about.

David

The charity Gingerbread, which merged with the National Council for One Parent Families, provides support to single parents and has a specialist advice service for lone parents caring for a child with an additional need. Contact details can be found on page 193. The organisation offers free fact sheets covering a range of issues that face single parents as well as information about support groups in your local area.

Internet support can work well if you are tied to the home by caring responsibilities. Through the internet you can get in touch with others who are at the same stage as you, as well as those who have come through relationship break-up and can offer helpful advice. Look for forums for single parents: some have sections for parents of children with special needs too, but often it is just a relief to 'chat' online to someone else going through the same thing.

For your security, and for that of your family as a whole, always be cautious about giving away too much personal information online – at least until you are confident you can entirely trust others on the forums and in chat rooms.

One popular site is www.specialkidsintheuk.org which has a members' forum, and www.singleparents.org.uk which has links to all sorts of local support groups.

COUNSELLING

Some people see counselling as a way of saving a relationship. It can also be a very useful tool in getting over a break-up.

I never considered counselling after my relationship broke down, I thought it was there for couples to try to save their marriages. I'm so glad I went, though, as I got chance to really be heard and share my story without being judged. I now realise that our child isn't the reason our relationship ended. Yes, her needs did put a strain on us as a couple, but there were already cracks appearing when I look back prior to her birth. I'd recommend counselling and think it should be offered as standard to all parents of children with an additional need.

Emma

If you feel that it would be helpful to speak to somebody about your relationship break-up you can contact your GP for a referral to a counsellor.

MEDIATION

Mediation can be a helpful way of resolving disputes after separation. A mediator supports couples to find their own solutions and come to an agreement regarding how to proceed. You will be asked to explain your concerns to each other in front of a qualified family mediator who remains impartial. You will never be told what to do but the mediator may suggest ways of resolving problems. They will be able to give you information about the law but do not give legal advice. You should see a solicitor for legal advice: the mediator may have a list of local solicitors who deal with divorce.

Costs of mediation will vary depending on the mediator used. Some also provide discounts for families on lower incomes and you may be able to get legal aid. For further information about mediation and to find out what is available in your area see page 195.

COLLABORATIVE LAW

Since 2005 there has been an alternative to mediation, called collaborative law. It is a non-adversarial way of securing a divorce agreement and it is becoming increasingly popular among couples who don't want to fall out irrevocably with each other and who want to maintain contact with their family.

It is different from mediation in that each has the support of their own solicitor throughout and there is a mutual focus of ensuring the best possible outcome for both sides. Basically, you pay a lawyer to help you, not to fight for you, so it can take the combative nastiness and stress out of a divorce.

LOOKING AFTER THE CHILD'S NEEDS

There are two important things for your child when your relationship breaks down. Make sure that your child knows that:

● They are still loved by both parents.

● The breakdown was not their fault.

The impact the situation will have on your child depends on how much your child understands, their age and how circumstances will change. If your child wants to talk about what is happening give them time and listen to what they are saying. Listen to their points of view if they are able to express them and answer their questions sensitively yet honestly. Your child does not need to know all the information about the break-up but they will benefit from knowing basic information and from being reassured that you both still love them.

Arguments

Do not argue in front of your child. This kind of behaviour is destructive and will undoubtedly cause them distress. Conflict between parents can be destructive for all children and should be avoided. Make it clear to your partner that you are not able to continue with a discussion that is getting out of control for the sake of your child. Try to say calmly, and without assigning blame, something like, 'I think we might be upsetting Mira. Can we talk about this tomorrow when she is at school?' Arrange to meet them at another time to continue the conversation in a calmer manner. Fixing up a specific time will ensure that the issue does not get swept under the carpet.

COMMUNICATING WITH YOUR EX

It is essential to communicate effectively with your ex if you are both going to be actively involved in the parenting of your child. When a child has an additional need there can sometimes be more to communicate, such as changes of medication or hospital appointment times.

Julie has found that taking the emotion out of the situation has helped and she and her children's father have achieved a more business-like relationship. 'There is no emotion,' she says, 'but we are most of the time respectful towards each other.'

Try to keep focused on what information you need to pass on. You may wish to write it down to remind you what needs to be said. If you have questions that you want to ask your ex-partner, jotting them down in bullet points might be useful to act as a reminder if you are feeling stressed.

Remember to treat each other with respect. You may no longer wish to be in a relationship with them but they are your child's other parent. Remind yourself that you are doing this for your child not for your ex-partner.

PRACTICAL MATTERS

If you are no longer living at the same home as your child you will need to organise access arrangements. It is best if this can be agreed between the two of you but if this is not possible you will need to take legal advice. If you are finding it difficult to come to an arrangement you could perhaps put something in place for a month and then review how it is working for all of you, including your child.

Your Citizens Advice Bureau will be able to give you contact details for local solicitors. Even if you weren't married and were co-habiting you may need to seek legal advice in order to sort out your finances and parental responsibility.

Parental responsibility is when a parent has responsibility for making decisions about a child's wellbeing and care. When you have parental responsibility you can make decisions about issues such as education, medical issues and housing. A mother always has parental responsibility for a child.

The situation is slightly more complex for fathers. A father will have parental responsibility if he is married to the mother. Since December 2003, a father has been granted parental responsibility if he registered the birth of his child jointly with the mother. Parental responsibility can be achieved for a father by making an agreement with the mother or by a court. All parents, however, have to provide financially for their child whether or not they have parental responsibility.

Finance will undoubtedly be affected when your relationship breaks down. Some couples choose to reach a private financial agreement while others use the Child Support Agency to calculate how much maintenance should be paid.

Help your finances go further

- Inform your council if you are the only adult in the household as you can be entitled to a reduction in council tax.

- Call the tax credits helpline to inform them of your new circumstances: your tax credits may go up if your income has fallen.

- You may be entitled to claim more benefits if you are living alone and/or your income has reduced. Speak to your local Jobcentre Plus or call their helpline.

INTRODUCING A NEW PARTNER

With time you may meet somebody new and establish a relationship. When your child has an additional need it can be more complex with your partner needing to learn about new conditions and a different way of life.

Julie's daughter is 14 and has cerebral palsy and learning difficulties. Julie is divorced from her daughter's father and is in a new relationship.

> Our relationship is just over nine months old and it is the first experience that my new partner has had directly with disability in a young person. Fortunately he is a very patient man. We have discussed how he is to approach my daughter and we agree that the main decisions, disciplines and so

On in respect of her will be mine to be made and he will act as support where needed. He is very supportive and open-minded and does things like fixing her computer, downloading songs for the MP3 player and other practical tasks.

Julie

Julie has invested time in speaking with her partner about her daughter's needs. The ground rules that they have set out help to ensure that the relationship works well. If you are beginning a new relationship it is important to speak to your partner about the difficulties that you may encounter and to discuss how you will approach these together.

My husband, who is not my son's father, can be less than understanding and quite critical. This puts me under a lot of strain.

Gail

Sometimes it takes time to appreciate the complexities of life when a child has an additional need and to become part of a family where this is the norm can be difficult for all parties. Refer back to the previous chapters for advice about how to communicate effectively. As we have seen throughout this book communication really is the key to successful relationship building.

IN SUMMARY

At times relationships do break up and it is necessary to move on. This chapter has given you advice about how to develop a support network around yourself at difficult times as well as how to look after your child's emotional needs. It is important that you do keep communicating effectively with your child's other parent despite your feelings towards them. This will in turn benefit your child. Remember to celebrate the positives about your own parenting and reinforce to your child that you love them very much.

9

Celebrating relationships

In this chapter

- Making new friends

- Personal qualities

- Other positives

- Strengthening a relationship

- Learning about disability

- Time to think

- Inspirational stories

While we have concentrated on the difficulties that parenting a child with additional needs poses, it is important to emphasise the positives. Although few parents would choose to enter the world of disability, it can have a positive effect on your life too, introducing you to people who you would otherwise never have met. It can also nurture qualities in parents making you more understanding of others, more patient and positive in outlook.

Parenting a child with additional needs can also strengthen your relationship as a couple. This chapter looks at celebrating your child or children with additional needs and shares stories from couples who feel that their relationship has been made stronger as a direct result of their child's difficulties.

Your life can be very different from how you planned when you become parents of a child with an additional need. Although you may take a different journey on life's path, it can still be a positive one.

> Life is different. Having a child with a special need puts your life in perspective. You are not as materialistic and expectations aren't as high. You enjoy the quality of life and have a different outlook on the world.
>
> Tracey

MAKING NEW FRIENDS

Parenting a child with an additional need can often lead you to mix in different and new social circles. Throughout this book parents have stated that they have found that their old friends have often not been able to fully understand their new situation and that old friendships have gone by the wayside. In contrast to this, new friendships are formed, often through school, support groups or even online forums.

Vicky's daughter Bethan has Down's syndrome. Since having Bethan, Vicky has found that her social circle has widened.

> Bethan has introduced us to people who I know will become lifelong friends of ours. We would perhaps have never crossed paths if we had not had her. Also she is a great icebreaker when out and about as she is such a happy, sociable child, she melts the hearts of everyone she meets.
>
> Vicky

Anne values the support of other parents who truly understand how she is feeling as they have been in similar situations.

> Try to find other parents who have been in the same boat as you. Emotional support is so important.
>
> Anne

Carol trained as a Face 2 Face befriender so that she could offer support to other parents. The training is delivered by a qualified counsellor and takes place over 40 hours.

> The training was quite daunting at first. For a long time I had been 'just Mum' caring for my child. It took some time to realise that my

experiences and views could be valuable to other parents. Our training group quickly bonded as we all had one thing in common: we were all parents of a child with a disability. In no time at all we were disclosing things within the group that we simply had not felt able to share with anybody else before. Some great friendships were formed during the training and we meet up regularly.

It is a great feeling to befriend others. I just wish that I had been able to access something similar after my son was born. I had a stream of practitioners visiting and endless hospital visits but nobody was really interested, or had the time or skills to ask how I was.

Having a befriender visit can really help parents. After all, the befriender really knows how it feels to have a child diagnosed with an additional need. It helps to reduce the feeling of isolation that parents may have and shows them that they will get through the difficult times and come out the other side. It is a difficult journey but there are people out there to support however they can. Many befrienders continue on to further education or to work in the area of disability. I have been truly empowered since becoming involved with Face 2 Face and now work for the organisation on a paid basis.

Carol

PERSONAL QUALITIES

Who you are as a person can change and develop as you face new challenges as a parent. When you develop new personal skills and qualities they can impact positively on relationships with your partner. You may appreciate them more and take less for granted. Many parents reported that they have developed good qualities as a result of parenting their child with additional needs. You may be more patient, learn how to take life at a slower pace and appreciate the small things.

> I really appreciate many of the things that other parents take for granted and am able to enjoy the wonder of my daughter's development. When she smiles at me, gives me a hug, pulls a funny face, it makes my day and all the other stuff melts into the background. My daughter is a complete joy.
>
> Sharon

Couples also highlighted ways in which their children have enriched their lives and made them more aware of the less superficial things in life.

> My son sees things so simply and so brilliantly, he has a brilliant mind. He is so full of enthusiasm to learn and to experience the world. He sees beauty, colours and things that we all miss.
>
> Shirley

Cheryl acknowledges the difficult times but says that despite these she has gone on to develop personal skills that enable her to manage stressful situations.

> I am so much more positive now and can cope under extreme conditions. We've got through the tough times with a smile on our faces.
>
> Cheryl

OTHER POSITIVES

Most parents of teenagers worry about their children getting into trouble as they go through adolescence. Jane tells us this is one worry that she won't have with her 16-year-old daughter, who has complex needs.

> The positives about parenting Isabelle are the unconditional love from her and knowing that at 16 I don't have to worry about her doing drugs, getting an ASBO or having an unwanted pregnancy.
>
> Jane

Anna's son is 16 and has Tourette's syndrome and obsessive-compulsive disorder.

> He is beautiful. I remember back to when he was a baby and forget about all the hard times and the pain he has suffered. He is such a lovely child and I'm so proud of him. There aren't any

negatives about my son. There are a few things I would change if I had my time again, but not regarding him, just other people.

Anna

Sometimes the additional need itself is the very thing that parents celebrate.

I wouldn't know where to start to tell you about all the positives. My son is extraordinary, quirky, eccentric, fascinating, brilliant and an incredibly funny child with an incisiveness of thought that is breathtaking and is largely the gift of his Asperger's.

Roberta

Keeping a special photograph album that shows your child's achievements can help couples to celebrate their successful parenting and strengthen their relationship.

STRENGTHENING A RELATIONSHIP

Some couples report that having a child with a disability has in effect strengthened their relationship. Angela says that she and her husband are overjoyed to have their daughter in their lives, describing her as 'very kind, beautiful and the embodiment of our love'.

A number of couples reported that they had to work as partners in order to offer their child the necessary care. This has meant that the relationship is in fact more of a partnership than before the birth. Lynn says that her child's complex needs have meant that she and her partner have had to work closely together, which has definitely strengthened their relationship.

We've had to learn to work as a team and in a way it has made us stronger. We try to get an hour each day together, even just to sit in the same room. On a Sunday we try to do something together as a family. Advice I'd give to other couples is work as a team, ask for help, stand back and trust the other to cope even though they might do things a different way. You must communicate: we have a whiteboard to write appointments on and what drugs he has. We also have a routine for each of us to follow so that I know that I'm responsible for our son until 3am and then my partner takes over. Get as much help from the outside world as you can – a cleaner, a volunteer, anything that makes your life easier.

Lynn

Rose agrees about the importance of teamwork in keeping the relationship strong.

Work together as a team and decide what is acceptable and both stick to it. It may feel uncomfortable at first but it helps the child know what the rules are. Mentally it is important to have a break so keep up with hobbies that interest you. When your partner comes home then go out sometimes to be with others and have normal conversations. It also gives your partner one-to-one time with your child.

Rose

Carol says she and her husband also find working together effective and they see themselves very much as a team. 'On Paul's days off he cares for the children so I can sleep a little longer,' she says. Carol clearly values this partnership approach, which has strengthened their relationship.

Sometimes it can be sharing simple activities that enhance couples' relationships. It is vital that couples get quality time together.

Do something together that will make you both laugh, whether that is playing board games, watching a comedy or having a blast at dance lessons. We did this and it was the best time we'd had together since we became parents, just laughing with and at each other. It reminded me that my husband is the same person I fell in love with and it was so nice to be with him away from

his 'worried dad' role. Make time each day just
for a hug, even if only when passing in the kitchen,
and remember to say 'I love you'.

Suzi

It is inevitable that at times you and your partner will disagree
over issues relating to your child. When this happens it is helpful
to discuss it so that resentment does not build up. A good strategy
to use is to begin with a positive before bringing up the issue and
to make sure that you end the conversation positively.

For example if you are disagreeing about how to manage behaviour
you could say, 'I really admire the way that you stay so calm when
Grace hits out. I think that we deal with this differently and we
perhaps need to discuss it as I feel it is an issue that you ignore
the behaviour while I try to implement our behaviour plan.' This
opens up the conversation in a positive way and feels much less
threatening than simply saying, 'I think that the way you ignore
Grace's behaviour is appalling.'

Once the conversation is drawing to a close give your partner
another positive such as 'Grace is so lucky to have a caring parent
like you,' so that your partner can see that you do recognise
their good points and that you are actively celebrating their
achievements as a parent.

Lots of couples found talking was a real positive in strengthening
their relationships.

You have got to communicate and keep time just
for yourselves. I have seen so many parents of
newly diagnosed children get so wrapped up in their

child's development that they forget to spend time together and this is so important. Yes, it is a very traumatic and emotionally draining period and people may feel they have to deal with their emotions by themselves, but you must not lose your own identity.

Take time out from being a carer and a parent and having some quality time as a couple without feeling guilty.

Jane

Try to make an effort to celebrate anniversaries in a special way. If you are struggling for childcare you could plan a meal at home or have a takeaway. The important thing is that you celebrate your relationship.

LEARNING ABOUT DISABILITY

A number of the parents we talked to admitted that prior to having a child with an additional need they knew little about disability. Some said they had gone on to set up support groups, aiming to empower other parents and pass on the knowledge that they themselves had learned over time. Other parents had taken a totally different career path and were now working in the area of children's disability as a direct result of their own child's difficulties.

TIME TO THINK

It can be hard to find moments to reflect in your busy day. If you get a chance, take some time out to reflect all the positives about your child, what they bring to your life that you wouldn't otherwise have. This can be in the form of new friends, or qualities that you feel that you now possess as a direct result of parenting a child with a disability.

Remember to celebrate the achievements not only of your child but for your family unit. For example, make time to celebrate your child achieving a new target at school. Make sure you acknowledge the role you as a parent have played in helping them towards their goal.

When you have attended a difficult meeting give yourselves a pat on the back for staying calm or putting your case across effectively.

Be positive

We don't often take time out to praise ourselves. Take a step back occasionally and tell yourself that you are doing a great job as a parent, or have done well to get through a tricky situation.

Give your partner support and rather than telling them what they are doing wrong, comment positively when they get it right. Tell them how pleased you were that they took the lead in the consultant's appointment and that you were proud of how they handled a difficult situation. When was the last time that you praised each other's parenting skills?

INSPIRATIONAL STORIES

Leanne and Charlie

Leanne Richardson's son Charlie is eight and has a diagnosis of an autistic spectrum disorder and communication delay. When she heard that the local authority had decided to withdraw all speech and language therapy for children aged five and over, Leanne decided to take some positive action.

I was so outraged that my non-verbal son was being denied the support that I knew he needed that I began to seek advice from voluntary agencies. I soon found out that our son's statement wasn't worth the paper it was written on. I was totally unaware that additional support needs such as speech therapy had to be written into the statement. I had presumed that education and health support were totally separate. I belonged to a local support group and decided to call a public meeting about the withdrawal of speech and language therapy.

This meeting was attended by parents, health workers and also a local county councillor and luckily she informed us of a health overview scrutiny meeting that was to be held in the next two days. About six other parents and I campaigned outside with placards. We then entered the meeting and one member was allowed to express our concerns.

I continued campaigning after having no response, appearing on local television and in newspaper articles. I decided to visit an independent speech therapist and this was the turning point for Charlie and for us. I actually got to see what speech therapy was. Cathy worked with Charlie on a one-to-one basis. No-one in the NHS had ever done that: their approach was to train me to work with him. We approached the independent therapist to initially carry out an assessment of Charlie but we saw some real improvements and continued to visit her on a weekly basis.

Leanne

Leanne and her husband took the local authority to a tribunal and won their case. Eventually the speech therapy service was reinstated but Charlie was without speech therapy for two years. Charlie now receives alternate group and individual therapy. Feeling let down by the system, Leanne decided to help other parents in similar positions.

I approached the National Autistic Society to see if they could support our group, Spectrum, in becoming a branch of their society. In June 2007 we launched ourselves as The National Autistic Society West Norfolk branch. I am now the branch officer and we have provided West Norfolk with several seminars, I really want to inform parents locally of their rights and to ensure that parents feel confident to challenge. The whole point is to empower parents and ensure that the mistakes that I made are not repeated. I didn't want other parents to battle like we had to. It was extremely emotionally draining.

The National Autistic Society informed me of a group of solicitors that provide workshops for parents and they agreed to help us. The event was attended by around 55 parents. It was free and also included a free one-hour consultation the following day if parents requested it.

Several parents have reported back to me saying that because of that workshop they now have speech and language therapy specified and quantified [in their statement of special educational needs]. They have grown in confidence and many have corrected the special educational needs caseworkers and quoted sections of the code of practice, which I think is fantastic. I believe the workshop gave parents confidence to challenge the local authority, which can be a very daunting task.

Leanne

Victoria and Joseph

In 2003, when Victoria Ballard's son Joseph was one, he was diagnosed with cerebral palsy. Unsure of what the future would hold, Victoria was very aware that she had to take each day as it came and did all that she could to help him.

I knew that I had to give Joseph as much encouragement and praise as possible. Improvement, however small, needed to be acknowledged. To help him on his way, I designed him a reward chart. It was simple to use, great to look at and showed obvious reward. The chart proved a huge success and constantly caught the eye of other mothers.

It was the combination of my developing role as a mother to a child with special needs and my professional skills as a graphic designer that led to the birth of the Encourage & Praise™ range of children's reward charts. The charts are designed so that parents and carers can tailor them to their child's specific needs allowing them to focus on the more demanding behavioural issues.

Five years on, I balance my life as a divorced mum to my two children (the breakdown of my marriage was nothing to do with my son's complications) and I continue to develop my range of charts, which can be found at www.encourageandpraise.com. Also we have now formed joint ventures working with top UK organisations producing bespoke charts for specialist requirements for children's health, education and general wellbeing.

The idea for the business came at a particularly difficult, low part of my life, but I truly believed in my product, it gave me hope and something to aim for. I am always forward focused and most importantly I never waste time on negative energy. I was in the situation and I had to make the most of it for my children. I truly believe that my business would not be the success it is today if I had not been so desperate for the concept to work and to bring some good from Joseph's cerebral palsy. Since starting my business I have been amazed at other mothers who have also set up small businesses. When exhibiting at parent and child shows so often the other exhibitors are mothers who have had an idea inspired by their children.

My biggest tip to any parent, whether your child has special needs or not, is make sure you have an interest for yourself. It will provide a focus and an escape and by doing this you will actually create a better environment for your children and, hopefully, for your partner. It doesn't need to be to the extent of running a business, just something that you enjoy. Something you can do in the evening when the children are in bed, such as learning a language, some form of study, or an aspect of art or craft. Helping a charity can be very satisfying too, particularly the one that supports your child's special needs and it will help keep you at the forefront of things too.

If you feel better this will feed on through to your children and to your partner. I liken it to the oxygen mask scenario — on a plane parents are instructed to put their oxygen mask on first, before seeing to their children. This demonstrates that you need to look after yourself first to be able to help your children.

Victoria Ballard, founder,
The Victoria Chart Company Ltd
Encourage and Praise reward charts

IN SUMMARY

It is important to focus on the positives of parenting a child with additional needs and the joy that this brings. Take some time out as a couple to reflect on how well you are doing not only as parents but also as partners. Celebrate your child's achievements, no matter how small they may seem. Keep your relationship alive by talking and enjoying activities together — and remember that you are also lovers and not just parents.

Useful contacts

SUPPORT ORGANISATIONS

Contact a Family

The only UK-wide charity providing advice, information and support to parents of all disabled children. Provides information about a full range of issues facing families including benefits, support groups and medical information.

0808 8083555

www.cafamily.org.uk

Face 2 Face

Befriending service specifically for parents of children with a disability. To find out about training as a volunteer or to see if you can access a befriender, visit the Face 2 Face website.

0844 800 9189

www.face2facenetwork.org.uk

Home-Start

A charity that offers support to families with young children.

www.home-start.org.uk

Mencap

Mencap's website has an excellent guide on how to make a will. Its learning disability helpline is an advice and information service for people with a learning disability, their families and carers.

0808 808 1111

www.mencap.org.uk

Sibs

The UK charity for siblings of disabled people. Offers sibling groups run by trained professionals such as teachers and social workers. Find out more about sibling support in your area or get information on how to support a sibling by contacting Sibs.

01535 645453
info@sibs.org.uk
www.sibs.org.uk

Sleep Solutions

Offers workshop training to parents around sleep issues. The organisation also offers a sleep advisory service in some locations. To find out about availability in your area contact Karen Hunt on 0844 800 9189 or by email at karen.hunt@scope.org.uk.

Sundowns

Support group for parents in Merseyside whose children have Down's syndrome.

0151 647 8888
sundownsoffice@aol.com
www.sundowns.org.uk

Sure Start centres

Families with young children are offered a range of services including day care and family support workers. To find your nearest centre visit the website.

www.surestart.gov.uk

COUNSELLING AND WORKING ON YOUR RELATIONSHIP

British Association of Counselling and Psychotherapy

Provides information about counsellors in your area.

Helpline 01455 883 335
www.bacp.co.uk

Couple Connection

An interactive site that will help you to strengthen your relationship.

www.coupleconnection.net

One Plus One

Research relationships and have an interest in supporting families and couples.

www.oneplusone.org.uk

Relate

To find out about Relate counsellors in your area visit the website.

0300 100 1234
www.relate.org.uk

Samaritans

Confidential non-judgemental emotional support, 24 hours a day for people who are experiencing feelings of distress or despair, including those that could lead to suicide.

08457 909090
www.samaritans.org

Carla Thompson, parenting skills consultant

MBACP accredited, UKRCP independent counsellor and psychotherapist based in Staffordshire.

01889 584926
www.ctcounselling.co.uk

Lynn Wilshaw, Relate counsellor

Lynn offers telephone counselling service or face-to-face counselling at her premises in Doncaster, South Yorkshire. Lynn also offers hypnotherapy and produces CDs to reduce stress.

01302 742820
www.lynnwilshaw.co.uk
www.hippohypno.co.uk (online store)

Joyce Wike, Relate counsellor
Based in South Yorkshire.

0122 620 0100

joyce.wike@btinternet.com

BEHAVIOUR MANAGEMENT

Encourage and Praise
A UK-based company specialising in reward charts.

08451 302 334

www.encourageandpraise.com

HOLIDAY INFORMATION

Break
Services include offering supported holidays, short breaks and day care for people with learning disabilities.

01263 822 161

www.break-charity.org

Calvert Trust
Offers purpose-built centres with a range of recreational activities; full board or self-catering.

www.calvert-trust.org.uk

Disabled Holiday Directory
An internet-based directory featuring wheelchair-accessible holidays.

01348 875 592
www.disabledholidaydirectory.co.uk

Livability Holidays
Part of a national charity providing opportunities for families including disabled people to go on holiday.

020 7452 2000
www.livability.org.uk

Tourism for All UK
Provides information regarding accessible accommodation.

0845 1249971
www.tourismforall.info

SUPPORT FROM CHARITIES

The Family Fund
Helps families with disabled children by offering grants to fund items that will make family life easier and more enjoyable.

0845 130 4542
www.familyfund.org.uk

Gingerbread

Support for lone parents, includes an information and advice line.

0800 0185026

www.gingerbread.org.uk

Ronald McDonald House Charities

RMHC was established in the UK in 1989 as an independent, registered charity supporting families with children in hospital. RMHC provides free 'home away from home' accommodation for the families of children requiring in-patient care in hospitals and hospices across the UK.

www.rmhc.org.uk

The Sick Children's Trust

A national charity providing 'home from home' accommodation for the families of sick children at specialist hospitals for paediatric care. The trust provides good quality, safe and secure accommodation for the whole family – free of charge.

info@sickchidrenstrust.org

COMPLEMENTARY THERAPY

CHIS-UK

A guide to complementary and alternative therapies.

www.chisuk.org.uk

To find a therapist contact the relevant body

General Osteopathic Council

020 7357 6655

www.osteopathy.org.uk

General Chiropractic Council

020 7713 5155

www.gcc-uk.org

The British Acupuncture Council

020 8735 0400

www.acupuncture.org.uk

The National Institute of Medical Herbalists

01392 426022

www.nimh.org.uk

Sarah Holland

An EFT practitioner and reflexologist based in Hertfordshire.

01462 621393

www.sarah-holland.co.uk

GOVERNMENT INITIATIVES

Common Assessment Framework (CAF)
www.everychildmatters.gov.uk/deliveringservices/caf/

Early Support
Aims to improve services for families with disabled children under five. Early Support is a way of working that keeps families at the heart of discussion and decision-making about their child.

www.earlysupport.org.uk

MEDIATION

The Family Mediation Helpline
Gives information about mediation and local contact details.

Helpline 0845 6026627
www.familymediationhelpline.co.uk

DOMESTIC VIOLENCE

Refuge

Offers help and support as well as a network of safe houses.

www.refuge.org.uk

Women's Aid

Works to end domestic violence against women and children.
helpline@womensaid.org.uk

www.womensaid.org.uk

Both organisations operate a joint free 24-hour telephone helpline:

0808 2000 247

FINANCIAL AND BENEFITS ADVICE

Tax credit helpline
0845 300 3900

Jobcentre Plus
0800 055 6688

EDUCATION

Portage

A home-visiting service for pre-school children who have additional needs.

www.portage.org.uk

Directgov

There is a section about special educational needs on the website.

www.direct.gov.uk

INDEX